GREAT
EXPECTATIONS

GREAT EXPECTATIONS

A Novel of Friendship

Bert G. Hornback

TWAYNE PUBLISHERS • BOSTON
A Division of G. K. Hall & Co.

30566

GREAT EXPECTATIONS:
A NOVEL OF FRIENDSHIP

Bert G. Hornback

Twayne's Masterwork Studies
No. 6

Copyright © 1987 by G. K. Hall & Co.
All Rights Reserved
Published by Twayne Publishers
A Division of G. K. Hall & Co.
70 Lincoln Street, Boston, Massachusetts 02111

Designed and produced by Marne B. Sultz
Copyediting supervised by Lewis DeSimone
Typeset in Sabon with Bodoni display type
by Compset, Inc., Beverly, Massachusetts

Printed on permanent/durable acid-free paper
and bound in the United States of America

First Paperback Edition

Library of Congress Cataloging in Publication Data

Hornback, Bert G., 1935–
Great expectations.

(Twayne's masterwork studies ; no. 6)
Bibliography: p. 147
Includes index.
1. Dickens, Charles, 1812–1870. Great expectations.
2. Friendship in literature. I. Title. II. Series.
PR4560.H6   1987   823'.8   86-29489
ISBN 0-8057-7956-6
ISBN 0-8057-8005-X (pbk.)

For Ernest and Eileen Sandeen

Contents

Note on References
and Acknowledgments

This book began with an invitation and an expectation. I was invited to write a book on *Great Expectations,* and expected to write it for serious students of the novel, avoiding as I did so "critical jargon" and all of that stuff called theory of criticism. I was delighted at the invitation—and I hope I have fulfilled the expectation.

I teach Dickens's *Great Expectations* every year at the University of Michigan. During the year in which I wrote this book I taught it three times: once to a group of high school students, and in two different university courses. I wish to thank all of the students in these courses for their contribution to the making of this book, particularly the students in my once-a-week *Great Expectations* minicourse. The students in this course heard an early version of this text in the form of lectures and responded in writing at the end of class each week. A selection from their responses is printed in an appendix to this book.

I also want to thank Rich Borer, Jonna Eagle, Tish O'Dowd Ezekiel, Tom Fredell, and Zibby Oneal for reading my manuscript and helping me with their generous suggestions and understandings. I am indebted to the trustees of the Wisbech Museum and to Jane L. Arthur, its curator, for allowing me to read the manuscript of *Great Expectations* and for permission to reproduce several pages of the manuscript for this book.

All references to the text of *Great Expectations* and other Dickens novels are to the Penguin editions of his works. The titles of the novels are abbreviated as follows:

PP   *Pickwick Papers* (1836–37)
OT   *Oliver Twist* (1837–38)

Citations unaccompanied by abbreviations refer to *Great Expectations*.

There is nothing more for me to say by way of introduction, except that having written this little book, I offer it to you with my own invitation and expectation. I invite you to join me in reading *Great Expectations* again, and I expect you to read it—as I do—with delight, with entertainment, with instruction.

Chronology: Charles Dickens's Life and Works

1812   Charles John Huffam Dickens born 7 February at Landport, Portsea, the second child of John and Elizabeth Barrow Dickens.

1817   Residence at Chatham, in Kent.

1821   Charles sent to school, in Chatham, to William Giles.

1822   John Dickens transferred to London in the autumn; Charles stays on in Chatham until the end of the school term, at Christmas.

1824   John Dickens confined in the Marshalsea Debtors' Prison for three months. Charles sent to work at Warren's Blacking Factory. In the autumn, Charles begins school at Wellington House Academy.

1827   Charles leaves school, and is employed as a solicitor's office boy.

1828   Begins work as a shorthand reporter at Doctors' Commons.

1830   On his eighteenth birthday, applies for a reader's ticket at the British Museum.

1831   Decides to become an actor.

1832   Teaches himself shorthand; becomes general reporter for the *True Sun* and parliamentary reporter for the *Mirror of Parliament*.

1833   First sketch, "A Dinner at Poplar Walk," published in December issue of *Monthly Magazine*.

1834   Reporter on the *Morning Chronicle*, a famous liberal daily. Publishes further sketches in *Monthly Magazine*.

1836   *Sketches by Boz* (February) is an immediate success. *Pickwick Papers* begins as a monthly serial on 31 March. Marries Catherine Hogarth on 2 April. Meets John Forster at Christmas.

1837   Birth of Charles, Jr., the first of ten children. Becomes editor of *Bentley's Miscellany,* and begins to publish *Oliver Twist* in its February issue. *Pickwick Papers* completed in November.

1838   Begins *Nicholas Nickleby* as a monthly serial in April. *Oliver Twist* ends in November; Dickens leaves the *Miscellany* four months later.

1840   Begins publication of a weekly magazine, *Master Humphrey's Clock*, including *The Old Curiosity Shop* as the main body of the magazine from April on.

1841   *The Old Curiosity Shop* completed in February issue of the *Clock*, and replaced by *Barnaby Rudge*, from the end of February until November.

1842   First visit to North America, January to June. Publishes *American Notes* in October.

1843   *Martin Chuzzlewit* begins as a monthly serial in January. Beginning of association with Angela Burdett Coutts in philanthropic and reformist causes of various kinds. Publishes *A Christmas Carol* in December.

1844   *Martin Chuzzlewit* ends in July. Dickens and family go to Italy, to stay for a year. *The Chimes* published as the second of his "Christmas Books" in December.

1845   Beginning of amateur theatricals, with Dickens as Captain Bobadil in *Every Man in His Humour*. For several months edits the *Daily News*; is succeeded by Forster. Writes articles against capital punishment. Publishes *The Cricket on the Hearth* in December.

1846   Publishes *Pictures from Italy* in May. *Dombey and Son* begins in October. *The Battle of Life* published in December.

1847   *Dombey and Son* ends in April. *The Haunted Man* published at Christmas.

1849   *David Copperfield* begins in May, in the usual monthly format.

1850   First issue of the weekly *Household Words*, "conducted by Charles Dickens," appears in March. *David Copperfield* ends in November.

1852   *Bleak House* begins in March.

1853   *Bleak House* completed in September. The first benefit reading of *A Christmas Carol* given in Birmingham in December.

1854   *Hard Times* published in weekly numbers in *Household Words*.

1855   *Little Dorrit* begins as a monthly serial in December.

1856   Buys Gad's Hill Place, in Kent.

1857   *Little Dorrit* ends in June.

1858   First of the professional readings, in London, followed by a tour of the provinces. Separates from his wife.

1859   First weekly number of *All the Year Round* appears in May, "incorporating *Household Words*." *A Tale of Two Cities* begins publication in *All the Year Round*.

1860	*The Uncommercial Traveller*, a series of sketches, published in *All the Year Round*, followed by *Great Expectations*, beginning in December.
1861	*Great Expectations* ends in August. Further readings undertaken, in England and abroad.
1864	*Our Mutual Friend* begins as a monthly serial in May.
1865	*Out Mutual Friend* ends in November.
1866	Reading tour of England, Scotland, and Ireland, extending into 1867.
1867	American reading tour begins in November, in Boston.
1868	Returns from America in April.
1869	Provincial reading tour begins in January; broken off in April because of ill health.
1870	Farewell season of readings in London, from January until March. *The Mystery of Edwin Drood* begins monthly publications in April; final number published posthumously in September. Dies at Gad's Hill on 9 June.

Charles Dickens, 1861
Photograph by John Watkins

One

Historical Context

Charles Dickens grew up into what was to become the Victorian world in the intellectual afterglow of Romanticism and the reformist spirit that had kindled the American and French revolutions. The years up to his twentieth birthday saw a number of major changes in English life. Reforms such as the emancipation of Catholics in 1829 and the political Reform Bill of 1832 made England a much more democratic nation, but they did not solve all its problems by any means. Indeed, they did not even address the huge social problems that the nation faced.

Victoria's motto as a child was "I will be good." But an ambition toward goodness was not good enough or wise enough in the complex world of nineteenth-century England. The great forces of the time were the Industrial Revolution and its by-products, Empire abroad and social upheaval at home. Victoria—by the grace of God Queen, Defender of the Faith, and (after 1876) Empress of India—gave her name to her world. But neither her authority nor her own determined goodness could solve its problems in any simple way.

In the decades before 1837 Romanticism had opened up—philosophically—the possibility of that greater good called the ideal which, once imagined, could be pursued. The spirit of revolutionary zeal which undertook that pursuit, however, was often blinded by its fiery passion. Looking back at the French Revolution from the mid-Victorian perspective of 1859, Dickens re-created its famous watchword as grim, rather than glorious: "Liberty, Equality, Fraternity—or Death" (T2C, 275).

There was no revolution in England. There were riots—rick-burnings on farms, machine-breakings in factories, protests in the streets, marches to Parliament Square even. But there was no social or political revolution.

What we call the Industrial Revolution had occurred, however, and it had indeed overthrown the old order in England, in the later decades of the eighteenth century and the first years of the nineteenth. By the beginnings of the Victorian age the new industrial world was in place, with its champions praising "progress" and preaching political economy. That the Industrial Revolution had uprooted tens of thousands of families and created masses of poor people living impossible lives in city slums—that those cities grew up simultaneously with their slums, as though there were architects trained to build that way!—were truths ignored by the economists and industrialists. "The greatest good for the greatest number" justified this kind of "progress"—and made Empire possible.

The Industrial Revolution created problems as much as it created what its advocates called progress. Dickens became one of the leading figures in the attack upon those problems. He began his public career as a novelist in the year before Victoria's accession to the throne; from 1836 until his death in 1870 his work was focused on social reform. Those who read his work—and he was the most popular serious writer in English history, in his time and ever since—were often the people whom in their personal and professional lives he attacked; but they continued to read him. J. C. Jeaffreson wrote, in 1858, of his influence on Victorian society: "His benefits to mankind are as innumerable as the flowers that cover the earth. . . . There is not a human heart in these islands . . . which Dickens has not at some time or other influenced for the better. . . . Among us there is not a grinding task-master who would not have been more selfish . . . had Dickens never lived to write. . . . We have been in his hands only plastic clay that he has fashioned. . . . We cannot . . . look out upon the world save through his eyes."[1]

Victorian England was a great society. What made it so was not just technological and scientific "progress," or the material wealth and power that enabled empire. The greatness of Victorian England was a cultural phenomenon more than a material or political one. Though the new national driving power was materialist, and the untitled mercantile barons seemed to care absolutely nothing for the lives of the "hands" whom they employed, the nation still had a conscience—and it responded to voices like Dickens's. The greatness of Victorian England was in part its self-consciousness, its self-criticism. The greatest of the Victorians were its social critics, finally, not its merchants or generals or empire-builders. And the greatest contribution to human history made by the Victorian age is marked by our calling it the age of social criticism.

Two

The Importance of the Work

Great Expectations was the thirteenth of Charles Dickens's fifteen novels. The novels that immediately precede it—Bleak House, Hard Times, Little Dorrit, and A Tale of Two Cities—are often called Dickens's "dark" novels because of the grim and seemingly pessimistic picture they paint of English society. Dickens was the great social critic among the nineteenth-century novelists (he invented the novel of social criticism, one might well say), and for many readers, both then and now, novels like Bleak House, and Little Dorrit were his greatest achievements.

But Great Expectations is also a novel of social criticism, and is one of the great achievements in the history of fiction. It is a brilliantly conceived attack on the vices that most threaten human society: selfishness and greed. Dickens had attacked these evils before, of course; as he saw it, "the arrogant and the froward and the vain" of this world "fretted and chafed and made their usual uproar" (LD, 895). The alternative to such noisy self-centeredness, he said, was "a modest life of usefulness and happiness" (LD, 895) that would work against selfishness and greed, and maybe even restore society. For Dickens, the connection between usefulness and happiness was "natural and rational" (DC, 331) as well as heroic.

In Great Expectations the hero is the novel's first-person narrator, Philip Pirrip—who "call[s] himself Pip" (GE, 35). The life of selfishness and greed that he exposes is his own. Having survived it—having learned usefulness and thus found happiness—he writes this novel, for us. It is a rich, complex work. It is often comic, as Pip the narrator looks back at his younger self and his adventures. It is often painful, too, as he reflects on the vanity and arrogance into which he fell.

Great Expectations is an indictment of the values by which our society conducts its often antisocial affairs. It is Dickens's first great frontal attack on the class society, an attack that he continues in his next novel, *Our Mutual Friend*. The values that Dickens affirms, in this novel as in all his other works, are those of friendship and love. More so than anything else he wrote, *Great Expectations* is a novel about friendship: about Pip's learning friendship. For Dickens, friendship is useful, and it brings—creates—true happiness. It is a relationship, however, not a possession—and there's the difficulty of it. Love is something you give—and give up.

At the end of *A Tale of Two Cities* Dickens's hero Sydney Carton gives up his life for his friend (and double) Charles Darnay: "It is a far, far better thing I do," he says, "than I have ever done before" (*T2C*, 404). No one in *Great Expectations* is asked to give up his life for his friend; the novel is not so melodramatic as that. Rather, the giving up in *Great Expectations* is carried to a spiritual and philosophical level. Joe Gargery, the simple blacksmith, articulates the idea: "Life is made of ever so many partings welded together" (*GE*, 246).

The greatness of *Great Expectations* is in that line. It explains the wonderful human drama Dickens has created as Pip's life, and given to us. If we understand what Joe says, we understand the novel—and we understand life the way Dickens would have us understand it.

Three

Critical Reception

When Dickens began to write *Great Expectations* he was full of confidence about his story. He spoke of it as "droll," rich in "humour," and "very funny."[2] The first reviews agreed for the most part that the novel was humorous. The *Times* found in it "that flowing humour . . . which disarms criticism, and which is all the more enjoyable because it defies criticism."[3] The *Athenaeum* called it "a tale of mystery and adventure," full of "such variety of humour, such deep and tender knowledge of the secrets of a yearning heart, as belong to a novel of the highest order."[4] The *Eclectic Review*, in a twenty-page essay, quoted at length the comic parts of the novel, including the whole of Wemmick's marriage scene. The *Eclectic* also found much in *Great Expectations* that was "thoughtful" and praised Dickens's "sympathy with humanity." It concluded with a condescending note of relief that "our author has not in this, as in most of his later work, set himself to the task of specially rectifying social sins and abuses."[5]

Not everybody liked *Great Expectations*, however. The *Athenaeum*'s calling it "the creation of a great artist in his prime"[6] was answered by *Blackwood's Magazine*, calling it "feeble, fatigued, and colourless."[7] The *Rambler* review concluded, "Perhaps, if he would lie fallow for a year or two, and let his thoughts range at will, and eschew everything that is tragic, sentimental, or improving . . . we need not despair of seeing a still more lively reproduction of the delightful absurdities with which he charmed his readers a quarter of a century ago."[8]

Most of the early Dickens critics liked *Great Expectations*. John Forster, Dickens's friend and biographer, praised it for its "subtle penetration into character," and likened it to *David Copperfield* while marveling at the way Dickens "kept perfectly distinct the two stories of a boy's childhood, both told in the form of autobiography."[9] He saw in Magwitch evidence of "Dickens's power of so drawing a character as to get to the heart of it, seeing beyond the surface peculiarities into the moving springs of the human being himself."[10] He argued that "Dickens's humour, not less than his creative power, was at its best in this book."[11]

Edwin Whipple wrote a long appreciation of *Great Expectations* for the *Atlantic Monthly* in 1877. Though he saw "much of Dickens's best writing in *Great Expectations*," he objected to the ending of the novel; and having read in Forster's *Life of Charles Dickens*, presumably, the original but discarded conclusion, preferred it to what he called the "unprepared, unexpected, and inartistic ending [that] . . . promised a marriage between the hero and heroine."[12] Whipple was particularly fond of Joe Gargery, and spent several hundred words discussing Dickens's success with him.

G. K. Chesterton, writing in 1911, approved of *Great Expectations*, though he saw it as "written in the afternoon of Dickens's life and fame." Still, it "has a quality of serene irony and even sadness," he said, "which puts it quite alone among his . . . works."[13] Chesterton argued at length about Pip's snobbishness, without ever distinguishing between Pip narrator and Pip character. "The study of Pip," he wrote, "is meant to indicate that with all his virtues Pip was a snob."[14]

George Gissing, the later Victorian novelist who admired Dickens greatly—as a social critic mostly—ignored *Great Expectations* in his *Critical Studies of the Works of Charles Dickens*, published in 1898. And though Ernest A. Baker wrote in praise of *Great Expectations* in his *History of the English Novel* in 1936, it remained one of the lesser Dickens novels, by reputation, until past the middle of this century. The novelist Ford Madox Ford, writing in 1939, loved *Great Expectations* and called it Dickens's "most serious novel." He found it "great" because of its seriousness, and because it was "not . . . founded on any conventional scheme of ethics, and . . . propounded no conventional solution to evils." He complained at its being ignored, and in a wonderful but exaggerated rhetorical flourish described the early response to it:

> The reviews fought shy of mentioning it; it was hush-hushed in such general conversations as the comfortable devoted to books; young ladies . . . counselled each other to avoid it. In official corners here and there it was even said, under the breath, that this was socialism.[15]

In our time *Great Expectations* has been acclaimed by one class of readers and scholars as the best of Dickens's work. They prefer it to novels like *David Copperfield, Bleak House, Little Dorrit,* and *Our Mutual Friend* in part because it isn't as big—as long—as those novels are. The big Dickens novels (*Pickwick Papers, Nicholas Nickleby, Martin Chuzzlewit,* and *Dombey and Son* complete the list) were originally published in twenty monthly parts each; their canvases are larger and more varied than that of *Great Expectations.* Instead of having twenty characters—and that's counting all the many Pockets—the big novels each have two hundred. *Great Expectations,* a weekly serial printed originally in Dickens's magazine *All the Year Round,* is not elaborated in the same way. The critics who prefer it over the longer novels do so not because it is shorter, but because they see it as so much better made. The form and structure of *Great Expectations* have been the subject of a number of essays in critical journals, and it has been an academic favorite because it is so "teachable."

For other readers and critics—the kind who are perhaps best identified as "Dickensians"—*Great Expectations* is not representative of Dickens at his best precisely because it is shorter, smaller, tighter in focus. It doesn't have so many characters, and its world is not so rich and full as the world of *David Copperfield* or *Bleak House* or *Our Mutual Friend.* They prefer—as Dickens did, for the most part—the "roominess" of the big books. No Dickensian would dismiss *Great Expectations,* of course, or fail to honor it as a brilliant and moving novel. But from Edgar Johnson's time on, in the heyday of Dickens criticism, as I scan through some fifty or sixty books on Dickens I find less attention devoted to *Great Expectations* than to the larger novels. There is still plenty being said about *Great Expectations*, however—and a great deal of it is very good. The best things written about it have to do with the social significance of the novel, the psychological depth of the characters, and the moral attitudes that Dickens develops. Thomas A. Jackson and Edgar Johnson both write about Pip's expectations as corrupting. They both argue that the novel is more than the story of Pip's "personal triumph over false social values";[16] it is an indictment of the great dream of Victorian—and for Jackson, modern capitalist—society. Johnson ends his strong and compelling essay citing the wonderful parallel between *Great Expectations* and Milton's *Paradise Lost*.

J. Hillis Miller ends his essay on *Great Expectations* at the same place, seeing Pip and Estella "accepting their exile from the garden of false hopes."[17] His reading of the novel is often psychologically interpretive—in the best sense—and he uses the imagery of the novel richly and effectively in developing his interpretation. He proposes Pip's relationship with Magwitch as his critical learning experience, and sees the conclusion of the novel—which for him is Estella and Pip's marriage—as growing directly out of that experience: "Once Pip has established his new relationship to Magwitch he is able at last to win Estella."[18]

Dorothy Van Ghent's focus is on the way "the Dickens world—founded in fragmentariness and disintegration—is made whole."[19] She works with the imagery of the novel, and with guilt and redemption as themes. Julian Moynahan has also written about guilt, devoting most of his attention to Pip's relationships with Miss Havisham and Orlick. Moynahan is one of the few critics who—like me—doesn't read in the end of the novel the expectation that Pip and Estella will marry. Indeed, for Moynahan *Great Expectations* "dramatises the loss of innocence, and does not glibly present the hope of a redemptory second birth for either its guilty hero or the guilty society which shaped him."[20] Pip, he writes, "cannot redeem this world. . . . Living abroad as the partner of a small, unambitious firm, he is to devote his remaining life to doing the least possible harm to the smallest number of people, so earning a visitor's privilege in the lost paradise where Biddy and Joe, the genuine innocents of the novel, flourish in thought-less content."[21]

Dickens's novels have attracted critics as much as they have attracted general readers over the years. More has been written about Dickens, in the scholarly as well as the popular press, than any other author. Modern Dickens criticism begins with Edmund Wilson's "The Two Scrooges" and George Orwell's essay in *Inside the Whale*, both published in 1941. Good pieces were also written before these two, like Jackson's *Charles Dickens: the Progress of a Radical* in 1938, and the *Dickensian* has often published significant material since its inception in 1904. But Wilson's and Orwell's works stand as landmarks. In 1951 Edgar Johnson's great biography, *Charles Dickens: His Tragedy and Triumph*, appeared. It is the single most important study of Dickens's life and work that has yet been published or is likely to be published. George H. Ford's delightfully readable and informative study, *Dickens and His Readers*, was published in 1955; John Butt and Kathleen Tillotson's *Dickens at Work*, a scholarly examination of Dickens's manuscript notes and plans, appeared in 1957. Hillis Miller's *Charles Dickens: The World of His Novels* was published in 1958. In some very real sense all of Dickens criticism since 1958 is indebted to these fine works.

In 1949 Humphry House began the immense job of editing Dickens's letters. In 1965 Oxford University Press began to publish the Pilgrim Edition of the letters, at the rate of something like one volume every five years. The Nonesuch edition of Dickens's letters contains 5811 letters; the Pilgrim edition, under the direction of Madeline House and Graham Storey, will eventually contain something in the neighborhood of twenty thousand. By the time the last volume is printed the ink in the early volumes may have faded entirely away. As of this writing, the Pilgrim volume that will contain letters from the years of *Great Expectations* is but a distant dream. George J. Worth's

Great Expectations: An Annotated Bibliography will be published in the Garland Dickens Bibliography series in 1987.

One of the marks of Dickens's enduring popularity is that there have been more than two hundred adaptations of his novels for the stage, and more than fifty versions produced as films for television. Peter Coe's deservedly unsuccessful 1985 stage version of *Great Expectations*, mounted by the Old Vic Theatre Company, was the sixth such adaptation of the novel; Minneapolis's Guthrie Theater—which stages *A Christmas Carol* annually—toured America with Barbara Fields's adaptation of the novel in 1985–86. There have been four film versions of *Great Expectations*.

Four

Dickens's Expectations

Great Expectations, Charles Dickens's thirteenth novel, was published in serial form in 1860–61. It was in some sense premature, in that Dickens had not planned to begin its publication so soon. He had just completed A Tale of Two Cities in October 1859, and that novel's final installment had appeared in his new weekly magazine, All the Year Round, in November of that year. A Tale of Two Cities had been succeeded by Wilkie Collins's The Woman in White, and that in turn had given way in September 1860 to a long, rambling narrative by Charles Lever called A Day's Ride. It took but four weeks for Lever's story to begin to hurt the magazine's sales—or so Dickens thought. A Day's Ride had "no vitality in it," he complained, and he was sure that it would ruin the circulation of his magazine if he allowed it to continue as the lead piece of fiction. He decided, therefore, to "strike in" with Great Expectations[22] and advertised it at the end of October as forthcoming. On the first of December the first two chapters appeared, replacing A Day's Ride on the opening pages of All the Year Round.

Dickens began what was to become Great Expectations as a short humorous sketch in early September 1860. While working on this "little piece" he found "such a very fine, new, and grotesque idea has opened upon me, that I begin to doubt whether I had not better cancel the little paper, and reserve the notion for a new book. . . . I can see the whole of the serial revolving on it, in a most singular and comic manner."[23] The serial form that Dickens had in mind for the expanded "little piece" was his usual twenty-part monthly serial. The failure of A Day's Ride, however, altered his plans, and he began to write Great Expectations for weekly publication.

In October he wrote to his friend John Forster, "The book will be written in the first person throughout, and during these first three weekly numbers you will find the hero to be a boy-child, like David [Copperfield]. Then he will be an apprentice. You will not have to complain of the want of humour as in the *Tale of Two Cities*. I have made the opening, I hope, in its general effect exceedingly droll. I have put a child and a good-natured foolish man, in relations that seem to me very funny."[24] He noted further that the "pivot on which the story [would] turn" was a "grotesque tragic-comic conception," but didn't explain what the conception was. And he concluded, "To be quite sure I had fallen into no unconscious repetitions, I read *David Copperfield* again the other day, and was affected by it to a degree you would hardly believe."[25]

Though Dickens regularly wrote several letters a day, he rarely wrote about his novels, and even more rarely revealed much about them before they were written. He would announce his determination to begin a new work, perhaps, or write to Forster about prospective titles, but seldom disclosed any of the particulars of his new story. As he worked, he would sometimes mention in a letter that he had just completed an installment, or that he was having difficulty getting one done, or that he liked what he was doing very much and expected friends to like it. But nothing more. The creation of characters and scenes occurred but once, on paper: and that was in the manuscript, which he sent, invariably much revised and blotted, to the printers.

Dickens's letter to Forster about *Great Expectations*—it came, according to Forster, with a copy of the first number—seems to tell us very little, except perhaps for that puzzling reference to the "tragi-comic conception that first encouraged [him]," and the remark about rereading *David Copperfield*. But almost everything important in or about the novel is mentioned, at least, in those few bare sentences: the first-person narrative, the connections between Pip and David, the humor, the "relations" in which he plans to put his hero and Joe Gargery, and that "grotesque tragi-comic conception . . . on which the story will turn."

We will come back to all of these, necessarily, as we proceed. First, however, I want to try to place *Great Expectations* in Dickens's career, and to comment on what we should expect of this novel, given the

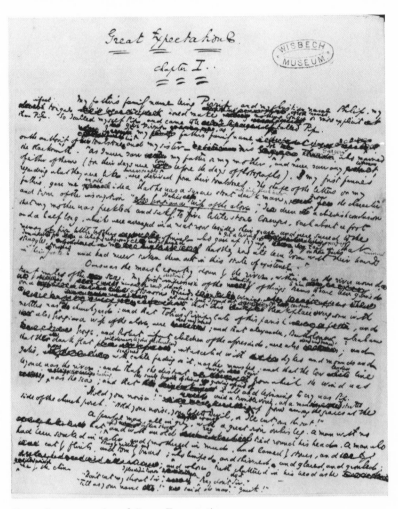

From the manuscript of *Great Expectations*,
courtesy of the Wisbech and Fenland Museum.

world in which Dickens was writing and his attitudes toward that world.

David Copperfield, that earlier first-person narrative which Dickens reread while working on *Great Expectations,* was published in 1849–50. It and *Great Expectations* are in a curious way the watershed novels of Dickens's career. In 1836, when the inital installments of *Pickwick Papers* began to appear, Dickens was an innocent young man of twenty-four. Though he had visited prisons and written about them, and knew something about the lives of the poor both from his own childhood experience and from his observation of the world around him, Dickens had not yet imagined the world he lived in. A quick look at *Sketches by Boz,* the collection of early pieces that Dickens had contributed to magazines before undertaking to write *Pickwick Papers,* will demonstrate the innocence of their author. He observes poverty and despair, but he doesn't feel it. He describes it, sometimes represents it dramatically even, but he doesn't imagine it, or create it in or with his imagination.

At the beginning of *Pickwick Papers* Mr. Pickwick is a congenial and naive sixty-five-year-old man who has spent his life in "the pursuit of wealth" (*PP,* 893). He has been quite successful in that pursuit, and proposes now to pursue experience: to engage with life itself. The first half of the novel is exquisitely funny, in a completely innocent way. But once Mr. Pickwick is sent to debtors' prison—for refusing to pay a judgment against him won by two shyster lawyers named Dodson and Fogg—the novel changes. The innocent fun comes to an end as Mr. Pickwick sees—and understands—the world before him. He tours the Fleet Prison and sees the existence that the poor debtors live there; and he retires, defeated by what he sees. "Henceforth," he says, "I will be a prisoner in my own room" (*PP,* 737). Eventually Mr. Pickwick buys his way out of debtors' prison, but the fun is over. For Dickens as for Mr. Pickwick, the world has changed. Dickens will never again see the world so simply, or so comically, as he had in the first half of this novel. At the end of *Pickwick Papers* the hero retires from the world, too old—and perhaps too frightened—to do anything about it. Sadly, he dissolves the Pickwick Club. He can't manage this world—

can't do anything about its madness. Experience has proved too much for him.

Dickens can't manage this world either. From *Oliver Twist* through *Dombey and Son*—from the novel following *Pickwick Papers* through the novel immediately preceding *David Copperfield*—he creates a number of young heroes and heroines whom he sends out into the world. But they can't find a way to survive in this world—or rather he can't find it for them—so at the ends of their novels they retreat, like Mr. Pickwick, to little pockets of love where according to their creator they live happily ever after, despite this mad world.

In *David Copperfield* Dickens creates as his central character a novelist: an artist, a man who uses his imagination to understand his world. David finds his role in this world, and through a reflective examination of both the world and his role in it he manages to survive in the center of it all, rather than retreating to some safe place in the unreal distances of fantasy-land.

David Copperfield is a great achievement for Dickens. David understands the madness of this world, but is not driven mad by that knowledge. Dr. Chillup, a simple, kind physician, worries that the "action of the brain" required in an artist's work may be dangerous: "Now, sir," he says, "about that brain of yours. . . . Don't you expose it to a good deal of excitement, sir?" (*DC*, 907). David ignores the question, even though it is repeated. He will not be driven mad, nor will he be driven away from the reality that he comprehends. His security in this world is his comprehension of it: his imaginative comprehension of it.

The imagination, for Dickens, is not something that lets us fabricate lies; rather, it lets us see the wholeness of the whole cloth. Imagination is that wise faculty through which we comprehend the otherwise confusing world around us. As Coleridge, the English Romantic poet, explained, the imagination "dissolves, diffuses, dissipates, in order to recreate . . . to idealise and unify."[26] We have to know the parts, the particulars of our world, in order to comprehend the whole of it. We analyze things—take them apart—in order to know them and their functions in the whole. Thus analysis has as its end the knowledge which tends toward re-creation. The artist, having looked analytically at his world, seeks to re-create its reality as understood reality. He proposes to give us an imaginatively comprehended world. That his imagination will "idealise" what it has seen—to use Coleridge's word—does not mean that it falsifies reality, but rather that it adds to reality what it has learned. The imagination is what enables us to make meaning out of life.

Dickens believed strongly both in this idea of the re-creative, meaning-making imagination and in the power of his own imagination. His struggle through the early novels is the struggle of his characters to survive in this world. Some die; others retreat or retire. Eventually some of them survive in it—but that is all they do. Dickens then realizes, it seems, that survival is not enough. We have to do more than survive life: we have to make life meaningful, and that requires imagination. His argument to himself is that if we can set as our ambitions to make meaning out of life, we won't be tempted—no matter how mad or bad that meaning may sometimes be—to run from it, or hide, or try to escape. Through our imaginative efforts we will become wise and will contribute our wisdom to our world. David Copperfield is the first of Dickens's characters to do this, giving us his "life" as meaning, as wisdom, as example. Appropriately, David's name is Charles Dickens spelled backwards—and he is an artist, a novelist.

But we are not all imaginative artists, and though Dickens continues throughout his career to argue for the serious imagination as our best resource for dealing with this world, he recognizes that David is a special—and specially endowed—creature. In the novels after *David Copperfield* we never again get an artist as a central character: Pip writes his own novel, but he is a businessman professionally, not an artist. In *Great Expectations*, as in most of his novels after *David Copperfield*, Dickens is testing whether common people like us can be so uncommon as to understand this world, if we try.

Insistently for Dickens, this world is a mad world. During the first half of his career—up to *David Copperfield*—Dickens regularly attacks evils he sees in it: the laws that create debtors' prisons and how such prisons are run, the New Poor Law and its workhouses, shameful schools and cruel schoolmasters, dishonest businessmen of various kinds and their dishonest business tricks. He attacks, too, the human vices that cause or allow these evils: pride, meanness, egotism, and greed. From the beginning of his career Dickens understands that public wrong has as its source private, personal fault. But his critical response in these early novels is always fragmentary. The closest he comes to a comprehensive statement of the problem we face is the narrative definition of "the world" in *Nicholas Nickleby* as "a conventional phrase which . . . signifieth all the rascals in it" (*NN*, 87).

In the novels after *David Copperfield* Dickens takes on "the world." Criticism of individual evils becomes criticism of social institutions; the criticism of individuals becomes criticism of society itself. At the same time, however, the individual is himself brought into much sharper focus; and whereas in the earlier novels frequently the problem faced by a character—the difficulty of a character's life—was the world and how to get on in it, in these later novels the problem that Dickens's heroes and heroines face is first of all themselves. Though Dickens attacks such antisocial social institutions as the law, government, and finally the whole idea of a class society in these later novels, the solution to the problem, as he sees it, lies always in personal rather than public revolution.

The 1850s was, as is often said, a "dark" decade for Dickens. The novels of those years—*Bleak House* (1852–53), *Hard Times* (1854), *Little Dorrit* (1856–57), and *A Tale of Two Cities* (1859)—are often called his "dark novels." They are angry novels, always on the edge of revolution. The narrative voice in *Bleak House* suggests the efficacy of "a great funeral pyre" or some other such convenience for the elimination of "the system," and *Hard Times* ends with a warning of "the Writing on the Wall." George Bernard Shaw called *Little Dorrit*, with its attack upon government, "the most seditious book ever written," and *A Tale of Two Cities* is about the French Revolution.

But revolution finally frightened Dickens. For him, the watchword of the French Revolution became "Liberty, Equality, Fraternity—or Death." However much he may have been tempted toward wanting to blow it all up, Dickens loved this world. Violent political revolution was violent, and therefore destructive. And the fault with this world, he believed, was not the world's, but ours.

In 1858 Dickens wrote to his friend and fellow novelist Wilkie Collins, "Everything that happens . . . shows beyond mistake that you can't shut out the world; that you are in it, to be of it; that you get into a false position the moment you try to sever yourself from it; and that you must mingle with it, and make the best of it, and make the best of yourself into the bargain."[27] It took Dickens twenty years and more of public life (*Pickwick Papers* began in 1836) to be able to articulate this idea, as an idea. He demonstrated it to himself–dramatized it successfully–first in *David Copperfield*. It is a major element of the argument of all the novels of the 1850s. And this idea is perhaps the abstract form of that "grotesque tragi-comic conception" which is the imaginative source of *Great Expectations*.

As a social critic, the mature Dickens writes against "the system." In *Bleak House* he attacks the law, particularly the Court of Chancery, as the institution representative of "the system." Chancery has "its decaying houses and blighted lands in every shire . . . its worn-out lunatic in every madhouse, and its dead in every churchyard." It "gives to monied might the means abundantly of wearing out the right," and "so exhausts finances, patience, courage, hope; so overthrows the brain and breaks the heart; that there is not an honourable man among its practitioners who would not give—who does not often give—the warning, 'Suffer any wrong that can be done you, rather than come here!' " (*BH*, 51).

Needless to say, those who work for "the system" see its workings very differently. One of its defenders, a lawyer called Conversation Kenge, presents his case for the system thus:

> We are a prosperous community, Mr. Jarndyce, a very prosperous community. We are a great country, Mr. Jarndyce, we are a very great country. This is a great system, Mr. Jarndyce, and would you wish a great country to have a little system? Now, really, really! (*BH*, 900)

19

And the narrative voice comments, in response: "He said this at the stair-head, gently moving his right hand as if it were a silver trowel, with which to spread the cement of his words on the structure of the system, and consolidate it for a thousand ages" (*BH*, 901).

The system in *Bleak House* works—or doesn't work—on the principle of "the perpetual stoppage" (*BH*, 211). Chancery specializes in "the perpetual stoppage." This infamously real court system is replaced in *Little Dorrit* by a brilliantly effective representation of the mythic Circumlocution Office, which specializes in red tape and "How Not To Do It" (*LD*, 145). Thomas Gradgrind, in *Hard Times*, thinks to solve problems philosophically, and goes to Parliament to do so. His philosophical scheme is Benthamite sociology, or utilitarianism; but as Mrs. Gradgrind tries to tell him, what is needed in this world is "something [that is] not an Ology at all" (*HT*, 225). For Dickens, what is needed is love: which is neither "ology" nor system nor institution. Love is what Sidney Carton dies for, at the end of *A Tale of Two Cities*. Love, Dickens argues, is the wisdom that can change—and save—this world: not revolution.

If we combine the critical perspectives of these four novels of the 1850s—if we align them so as to discover their common themes and arguments—we will find first that the conflict is between the rich and the poor, and second that Dickens's imaginative focus is more on how to resolve that conflict than on the conflict itself.

When Oliver Twist asks for "more" (*OT*, 56) he articulates the Ur-phrase of all social revolution, and begins Dickens's career as a social critic. Anthony Trollope, a contemporary fellow novelist, wrote at Dickens's death that he was "a radical at heart."[28] This is true, if we think of "radical" in its proper sense of reference not to fringe or extreme thoughts and activities, but to roots: to origins, sources, centers. (A radish is a root vegetable; to find the square root involves radical mathematics.) Dickens's radicalism means that, in *Bleak House*, given that "the system" won't work, he chooses as his solution to the problem, not "blowing up" Chancery but Esther Summerson's determination "to be as useful as [she] could . . . to those immediately about

[her]; and to try to let that circle of duty gradually and naturally expand itself" (*BH*, 154). In *Hard Times* Dickens sees the Utilitarian philosophy as ignorant, first, and then perverse. "The greatest good for the greatest number" is a useful idea for those in charge of the distribution of that "good." They peg the point of alleged balance. The very greatest good turns out to be available to but one of us. The good that we call luxury can be enjoyed by a few more, perhaps, and a modest, comfortable good by a great many. But all of this good is made possible by the toil and suffering of the great mass of humanity, whose only comfort, presumably, lies in the creation of good for the rest of us.

The pyramidal structure of Utilitarian philosophy was not a new invention; Jeremy Bentham merely adapted an ancient idea to the justification of "progress" in the Industrial Revolution. The "hands" of Coketown do the work, and the rest of us enjoy the progress. For Dickens, this state of society is neither success nor progress; it is "Hard Times"—and he sees, he claims, "the Writing on the Wall" (*HT*, 313), unless we learn our "duty."

By the time Dickens gets to *A Tale of Two Cities*, in 1859, he has brought his understanding of the failure of our society to a crisis point. He has achieved this painful understanding through his imaginative creation of the fictional realities that we call *Bleak House, Hard Times,* and *Little Dorrit*. But even though he finds realistic ways in these novels for good people to live in this world—to survive in the midst of social failure, and work for change—he is neither relieved nor satisfied. "I have a grim pleasure," he writes early on in the composition of *Little Dorrit*, "in thinking that the Circumlocution Office sees the light," and he "wonder[s] what effect it will make."[29] But what he writes seems to have no effect at all: even if they—we—see the light, that seeing appears to make no difference.

To relieve his frustration with this reality, Dickens turns away from the present, to mythic times. *A Tale of Two Cities*, set in the years of the French Revolution, is a historical fiction. But historical fictions—good ones—are always about the present, not the past; and thus *A*

Tale of Two Cities is, from its well-known opening sentence on, a mythic novel about this present world:

> It was the best of times, it was the worst of times, it was the age of wisdom, it was the age of foolishness, it was the epoch of belief, it was the epoch of incredulity, it was the season of Light, it was the season of Darkness . . . in short, the period was so far like the present period. . . . (*T2C*, 35)

On one level *A Tale of Two Cities* is about the revolution, and the war between the peasant class and the aristocracy. Dickens recognizes as he writes about this conflict that the supremacy of one class—either class—over the other is no solution at all. In showing himself this fact so graphically—in creating it, imaginatively—he discovers a new focus on the problem and a new way of seeking its solution. The new focus is on the idea of a class society; and the new way of seeking the problem's solution is to create characters who can get beyond the limitations and divisions of class identification and see themselves as responsible humans.

By the end of *A Tale of Two Cities* Dickens is no longer concerned about the revolution and its evils. He knows—from imaginative experience, now—that political revolution is destructive and perverse, because it is ignorant. He concludes the novel with Sidney Carton's wise and beautiful death. Sidney has found a purpose in his life, at last; and he performs the ultimate act of generosity in giving up his life to save Charles Darnay's. This act has nothing to do with the revolution, or two cities, or class. It is an act, however, that Dickens believes could change—and save—this world. Thus, as Carton faces death, Dickens imagines prophetic last words for him:

> I see Barsad, and Cly, Defarge, The Vengeance, the Juryman, the Judge, long ranks of the new oppressors who have risen on the destruction of the old, perishing. . . . I see a beautiful city and a brilliant people rising from this abyss, and in their struggles to be truly free, in their triumphs and defeats, through long years to

come, I see the evil of this time and of the previous time of which this is the natural birth, gradually making expiation for itself and wearing out.

I see the lives for which I lay down my life, peaceful, useful, prosperous and happy. . . . I see that I hold a sanctuary in their hearts, and in the hearts of their descendants, generations hence. I see her, an old woman, weeping for me on the anniversary of this day. I see her and her husband, their course done, lying side by side in their last earthly bed. . . . I see that child who lay upon her bosom and who bore my name, a man winning his way up that path of life which once was mine. I see him winning it so well, that my name is made illustrious there by the light of his. . . . I see him, foremost of just judges and honoured men, bringing a boy of my name . . . to this place—then fair to look upon, with not a trace of this day's disfigurement—and I hear him tell the child my story, with a tender and faltering voice.

It is a far, far better thing I do, than I have ever done. . . . (*T2C*, 404)

"Everything that happens . . . shows beyond mistake that you can't shut out the world; that you are in it, to be of it . . . and that you must mingle with it, and make the best of it, and make the best of yourself into the bargain." Carton does this: makes this "best," lives—and dies—by its truth, for Dickens. In doing so he sets up, perhaps, the "grotesque tragi-comic conception" from which *Great Expectations* grows.

Earlier I called *Great Expectations* the second "watershed" novel (*David Copperfield* was the first) in Dickens's career. In *David Copperfield* Dickens created the imaginative character, the artist, who could survive in the world by comprehending it. Though it is important for David to come to know himself—"to get a better understanding of [him]self" (*DC*, 890)—the main focus of the novel is on David's coming to know the world around him. Thus *David Copperfield* is a novel "about" David in both senses of the word.

In *Great Expectations* the main focus seems to be on Pip's learning himself. The self-criticism that pervades Pip's narration of his life is sometimes almost overwhelming: Pip dislikes his younger self so much, sometimes, that we have difficulty remembering that our narrator is that young snob, matured. *Great Expectations* is a novel about Pip's creating and then re-creating—reforming—his identity. He does this, of course, in a social context: we all grow up influenced by the world we live in, and by the conflicts and choices that it presents to us.

From the beginning, the world seems to be against Pip. He is on his own, alien, an orphan "brought up by hand." His existence seems precarious, given the hostility of the world around him. His identity is nothing more than a diminutive self-definition: he "call[s] [him]self Pip, and [comes] to be called Pip." His parents are "dead and buried," as are his five little brothers, "who gave up trying to get a living, exceedingly early in that universal struggle." His "first most vivid and broad impression of the identity of things" (435) is that this world is unfriendly at best to lonely little boys; and he sees himself, then, as but "a small bundle of shivers, growing afraid of it all and beginning to cry" (36).

Because the young Pip sees himself as alien and thus on his own in this world—he can't understand at this point the significance of Joe's survival, let alone Joe's goodness—he is on the lookout for ways to achieve security. The first that proposes itself to him is wealth; the second is knowledge. The knowledge Pip seeks, however, is not sympathetic understanding, but sophistication—which might somehow lead to wealth. When it comes to learning, Pip would rather not "call Knaves at cards Jacks," and he wants to learn how to avoid having coarse hands, and wearing thick boots (99).

Pip is a setup for "great expectations." To escape from his small world—from the precariousness of the diminutive self-definition he is stuck with—Pip longs to rise in status and significance, manners and class, to be a "gentleman." And when lawyer Jaggers proposes that he "be brought up a gentleman—in a word, as a young fellow of great expectations" (165), he is ready.

Once we realize that Pip's ambitions create the focus for the novel we can revise our understanding of the opening chapters. They seemed originally to be about Pip's simple, childish attempt to survive in this terrible and threatening world. But the conflict of those first chapters is in fact a conflict of class. To Mrs. Joe, Pip and Joe are inferior creatures. Mr. Pumblechook, "who drove his own chaise-cart" (55), is the important character in Mrs. Joe's world, and on Christmas Day, with the silver paper removed from the parlor furniture and "the front door unlocked . . . for the company to enter by" (54–55), class—or the pretense to class—is what's important.

It is as *Great Expectations* becomes a novel about the class society that it becomes the second "watershed" novel of Dickens's career. In *David Copperfield* Dickens teaches himself and us how we can survive meaningfully in this world, by comprehending it; and David shows us how such comprehension of the world is the beginning of the critical act of changing—and saving—it. In *Great Expectations* Dickens teaches himself and us that this world goes wrong because we go wrong, and that to change this world for the better we must first change ourselves.

Late in *David Copperfield* David argues to his young wife Dora that there is a "contagion" in them: "We infest everyone about us," he says; "we incur the serious responsibility of spoiling everyone who comes into our service, or has any dealings with us." Sensing that he and Dora are a "corrupting" influence, he says: "I begin to be afraid that the fault is not entirely on one side, but that these people turn out ill because we don't turn out very well ourselves" (*DC*, 760–61). In *Great Expectations* this argument is generalized, and Pip finally comes to see himself, in his desire to be a gentleman, as the representative source of corruption in a corrupt world.

The redefinition of what it means to be a gentleman which *Great Expectations* finally produces, as the result of Pip's self-criticism, is the source of Dickens's last complete novel, *Our Mutual Friend*, and even the germ of the brilliant final production of his pen, *The Mystery of Edwin Drood*. "Gentleman" is not a word that refers to class, ancestry, or occupation. To be a gentleman, one must have a gentle soul—as

Joe does. And in presenting Pip's argument of this idea, Dickens turns the focus to "metaphysical" (*GE*, 100) considerations, and invites us to consider directly what things—and people—are made of.

Dickens began his career by sending Mr. Pickwick out to see the world: to make "journeys and investigations" and "observations" of all sorts (*PP*, 68). What Mr. Pickwick saw disturbed and frightened Dickens. Once he overcame his fear—learned the world's evil, and thus secured himself against it—he began a large and comprehensive attack upon it. And then, at the height of his frustration with this chaotic and unjust world, he turned his critical attention from it to us. What he saw came from what we are. Like Pogo, Walt Kelly's famous possum, Dickens would say "We have met the enemy—and he is us."

Five

Pip's Story: The First-Person Narrative

When you see a first-person narrative, you have to start by asking it questions immediately. The first one you ask—and the second, probably, and the third, and maybe the last one, finally—is "Why is this a first-person narrative?"

There are a great many first-person narratives in our cultural tradition. The ancient Greek historians wrote first-person narratives: Herodotus and Thucydides both begin their histories with assertions of their own identities. "I, John . . . " is the witness statement in the Book of Revelation in Christian mythology. Dante's *Divine Comedy* is importantly a first-person narrative, in which Dante character's story finally catches up with Dante narrator, at the top of Paradise. Shakespeare's most famous characters all do segments of first-person narratives, called soliloquies. Wordsworth's most famous poem, *The Prelude*, is written from this perspective as "the growth of the poet's mind." *Moby-Dick* begins, "Call me Ishmael," and Ralph Ellison's great modern novel begins with the sentence "I am the invisible man." Even *The Catcher in the Rye* is a first-person narrative, though Holden Caulfield assures us in the first sentence he writes that he is not going to tell us "all that David Copperfield kind of crap."

One might even argue that the egocentricity of this latter quarter of the twentieth century is a first-person orientation—except that egocentricity is different from first-person narration. First-person narratives, in literature, are reflective rather than egocentric. The "me" generations, when they talk about themselves, assume their own importance. First-person narratives assume that the self—the self-at-the-center—has to learn both the world around it and itself. The first-person narrator tells a story. The egocentric character has no story to

27

tell: he exists, isolated by his own assumed importance in the onanistic moment of self-conception.

When you ask a first-person narrative why it is such, perhaps the first answer you get is one concerned with what gets called "identification." "It's easy to identify with Pip," one says, "because he is telling his own story." If that were true—if there were a real advantage to first-person narrative, created by the idea of identification with the narrator—then surely most if not all fictions would be told from that point of view. Surely Homer—that greatest of all storytellers—would have written first-person narratives.

But such is not the case, so we will have to ask again: "Why is this a first-person narrative?" It may take us all the way to the end of our discussion of *Great Expectations* to answer this question fully, but we can start here with some preliminary work toward the answer.

The focus of most serious fiction, from Jane Austen to James Joyce and beyond, is a moral one. The narrative voice embodies certain values, typically, and from the moral perspective that these values create or articulate, the narrative voice teases and tests the central character, pushing him toward an understanding and acceptance of those values. The dramatic tension of the story derives from this conflict or learning confrontation. The resolution of the conflict—in the central character's learning or not learning his lesson—is the moral achievement of the novel.

First-person narratives work a bit differently from other novels, simply because we know, from the beginning, that the conflict between the narrator and the central character must be resolved positively. The narrator is the central character grown up. It is hard to tell a story well if you don't know what it means; it is even harder to tell your own story well if you understand neither it nor yourself. The assumption with which we begin a first-person narrative, then, is that the narrative voice knows—or will know, through the story's telling—the significance and meaning of the story.

Sometimes what the narrator learns or knows from his autobiographical endeavors may not be very enlightening or satisfactory. Norman Mailer's early novel *Advertisements for Myself* is appropriately titled for an act of fictional egotism: the value in advertisement is a shoddy one at best. Most political autobiographies are self-serving, by definition. One European reviewer of Henry Kissinger's *The White House Years* referred to it as "The White-Wash Years," and the joke took a firm hold in readers' minds. Gerald Ford's autobiography, *A Time to Heal*, contains at least one piously framed lie—about a "protestor" at a commencement address, who was in fact planted by Ford's agents[30]—which, for any intelligent reader, must undermine Ford's claim of honesty and personal integrity as the marks of his brief presidency.

Though some autobiographies—fictional or otherwise—are unsatisfactory because they are self-serving, the great autobiographies are in fact great because, generously, they serve us at self's expense. Dostoyevski's Underground Man writes, painfully, at the end of the first section of *Notes from Underground*, "So why, for precisely what reason do I want to write?"[31] Toward the end of *Invisible Man* the narrator asks, "So why do I write, torturing myself to put it down?"[32] His answer is that "in spite of [him]self [he has] learned some things." The mind, he says, knowing itself—discovering its meaning in this world—has a "social responsibility."

Pip's narrative exposition of his own life begins comically—but only because we know that the Pip who survived this childhood is telling the story, and can smile at it as he tells it. The situation remembered is not comic; but the act of remembering can make it so. Thus we can laugh when as Magwitch asks Pip, "Where's your mother?" and Pip replies, pointing, "There, sir!" Magwitch jumps with fright—though the boy Pip hardly laughs at Magwitch's error. And when Magwitch tilts Pip over so far that he says, "If you would kindly please to let me keep upright, sir, perhaps I shouldn't be sick," he isn't being clever or intending to make a joke; but his narrator self sees the humor in the whole situation. He extends it in reporting Magwitch's response to his request: "He gave me a most tremendous dip and roll so that the church jumped over its own weather-cock" (37).

For the child Pip these experiences were terrible, and terrifying. The narrative recollection of them, however, presents them as comic and grotesque, and reveals to us what the child Pip could never have seen at the time: that Magwitch is as miserable and terrified as Pip is himself.

As the novel progresses, this accidental meeting on the marshes becomes not only the literal source of Pip's "great expectations," but also the symbolic source of or model for his reidentification. Both connections are ironic, the first because Pip expects his expectations to come from a socially acceptable source, the second because Pip—terrified of the idea of a convict—has no intention of finding himself identified with such a creature as Magwitch.

The child Pip is unable to see the corruption of Miss Havisham and is pleased to dream of her being the source of his expectations. He already knows, of course, from Mrs. Joe's example, what class differences are—how silly they are—and he understands that as far as his sister is concerned he and Joe are at or near the bottom of whatever class ladder there is. But this knowledge doesn't bother Pip or interfere with his own thinking about class, because he has no respect for his sister. Thus when he meets Miss Havisham, he is immediately seduced by the idea of wealth:

> I entered . . . and found myself in a pretty large room, well lighted with wax candles. . . . It was a dressing-room. . . . [P]rominent in it was a draped table with a gilded looking-glass, and that I made out at first sight to be a fine lady's dressing-table.
> . . . She was dressed in rich materials—satins, and lace, and silks. . . . Some bright jewels sparkled on her neck and on her hands, and some other jewels lay sparkling on the table. . . . [H]er watch and chain were not put on. (87)

It is gold, here, that attracts Pip—even before he sees Estella. What first attracts and seduces him is the glitter of riches. He notices, he says, all of this "rich" and "bright" and "sparkling" finery almost immediately: "It was not in the first few moments that I saw all these things, though I saw more of them in the first moments than might be supposed" (87). And when Estella comes in, carrying a candle "like a star" (89), she completes the seduction. Her haughty disdain for him is "infectious" (90), and for the first time he sees himself as "coarse," "common," and "vulgar." In his humiliation and self-deprecation, Pip wishes that "Joe had been rather more genteelly brought up," for "then I should have been so too" (92).

This first visit to Miss Havisham's marks the beginning of Pip's downfall, and it is represented seriously and painfully by the remembering narrator. As he re-creates in his memory Estella's insolence toward him, the remembered hurt upsets his present equilibrium, and he has difficulty defining the experience: "I was so humiliated, hurt, spurned, offended, angry, sorry—I cannot hit upon the right name for the smart—God knows what its name was" (92).

When the boy Pip gets home, however, he retells his experience at Satis House quite differently. He is too proud to confess his hurt, especially to critical and unfriendly ears, and is in "dread of being misunderstood" by Mrs. Joe if he relates his strange adventure to her. By the time Pumblechook arrives, "preyed upon by a devouring curiosity," Pip's mood has shifted. Pumblechook's fascination with the idea of "up town" (95)—his obvious seduction by his own fantasies of how the wealthy might live—turns Pip into a brilliant comic liar. He leads Pumblechook on, and his sister as well, with a wonderful burlesque of what he has seen. His story is "lies," as he later admits to Joe (99); but it is "lies" born out of awkward truths—and therein lies the burlesque.

Once Pip realizes that Pumblechook has never seen Miss Havisham—which he discovers as soon as he describes her—Pip lets his imagination run free. And freed, Pip's imagination tells a deeper truth about him than the comedy of the scene would have us expect. In his marvelous re-creation of his afternoon at Satis House, Miss Havisham sits "in a black velvet coach," eating "cake and wine" from "a gold plate." He and Estella have "gold plates," too, though Pip is sent, like a servant, "up behind the coach" to eat. Four dogs eat out of "a silver basket," and he almost invents "four richly caparisoned coursers" to pull the velvet coach (97). When the three of them—Pip, Estella, and Miss Havisham—play, they wave flags, "a blue flag, and . . . a red one . . . [and] one speckled all over with little gold stars" (97–98).

> "And then we all waved our swords and hurrahed."
> "Swords!" repeated my sister. "Where did you get swords from?"
> "Out of a cupboard," said I. "And I saw pistols in it—and jam—and pills." (98)

The grand fabrication winds down, and the marvelous burlesque ends. Pip's imagination has been telling the truth, of course: the velvet coach and the gold plates and the silver basket and the gold stars are all translations into myth of the rich glitter that took possession of Pip's mind when he first entered Miss Havisham's room. When his imagination runs down, at the end of his fantastic story, it still tells the truth, cryptically, in little-boy language. The cupboard that contained "swords" and "pistols" also contained, he says, "jam—and pills." Jam comes, I suspect, from the little boy's reality: that is what he would really expect to find in a wonderful cupboard. And pills? His finding pills there is his way of saying "That lady is sick, or crazy."

When Pip admits his "lies," Joe asks, "What possessed you?" And Pip replies, "I don't know what possessed me" (99). The verb, here, is an important one. Possession is always a bad thing, in the world of this novel, whether the reference be Wemmick's to the value of "portable property," or Magwitch's to being Pip's "owner" (339) and his plans for the love that "money can buy" (338) for his boy. And though the boy Pip can't quite answer Joe's question here, the narrator knows what has "possessed" him: it is wealth, and the sordid idea of class distinction.

Pip is unhappy at being a "common" boy (99). This complaint about his identity constitutes "a case of metaphysics," the narrator says, as far as his child-self is concerned. But Joe knows better: it is not Pip's identity that is wrong, but his attitude toward himself and toward his world. And Joe takes "the case altogether out of the region of metaphysics" (100) with this insight.

In the beginning of the novel Pip narrator tells us of his self-identification as "Pip," and of his "first most vivid and broad impression of the identity of things" around him. The narrator's organization of those opening paragraphs emphasizes Pip's aloneness and alienation, and his child-self's sense of the precariousness of his existence. Life is referred to as "that universal struggle" which claimed all of Pip's siblings "exceedingly early" (35); and to the boy sitting there in the graveyard "the identity of things" seems to promise little of hospitality for the future.

There is nothing wrong with Pip's identity, except for a morbid self-pity that makes the worst of things and sees the worst in the world around him. Instead of being metaphysical, Pip's problem is "lies" of all sorts—and "lies," says Joe, "is lies" (100):

> Lookee here, Pip, at what is said to you by a true friend. Which this to you the true friend say. If you can't get to be oncommon through going straight, you'll never get to do it through going crooked. So don't tell no more on 'em, Pip, and live well and die happy (100-101).

Pip's unhappiness with who he is comes from his loneliness and sense of alienation. The distortion that results from morbid self-absorption is what causes him first to misperceive things and then to lie. He misperceives both himself and the world around him, and by lying perverts himself and misrepresents the world.

We see Pip's misperception of himself in his adopting Estella's "infectious" disdain for him: "I had never thought of being ashamed of my hands before; but I began to consider them a very indifferent pair" (90). "I took the opportunity," he says, "to look at my coarse hands and common boots. My opinion of these accessories was not favourable. They had never troubled me before, but they troubled me now, as vulgar appendages" (91–92).

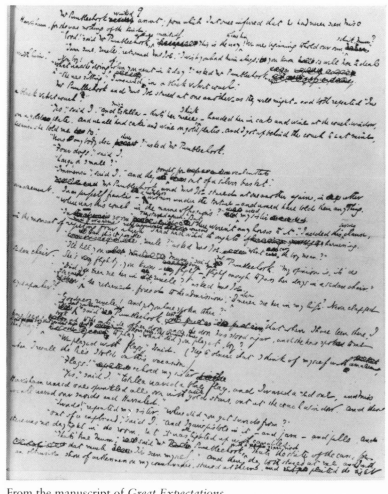

From the manuscript of *Great Expectations*,
courtesy of the Wisbech and Fenland Museum.

Pip's misperception of the world around him causes him to under-value his relationship with his "true friend" Joe, and think of himself as alone. His parents are "dead and buried" (35), and Mrs. Joe would rather not be his sister. He despises his Uncle Pumblechook, who isn't really his uncle anyway. But Joe, his brother-in-law, is his friend in fact, and insistently so, despite Pip's condescension and later neglect. Pip wants something more than Joe's friendship, however; he wants—as soon as he meets them—to be related to Miss Havisham and Estella. He quickly decides that he is "in love" with Estella, and then creates in his mind the dream that Miss Havisham has befriended him, and will provide for him.

Pip's real lover is Joe, who is "ever the best of friends" (78). And the man who provides for him is Abel Magwitch, the convict, who takes the name "Provis" as his disguise.

At the end of the chapter in which Pip tells his "lies" his narrator self writes:

> That was a memorable day to me, for it made great changes in me. But, it is the same with any life. Imagine one select day struck out of it, and think how different its course would have been. Pause, you who read this, and think for a moment of the long chain of iron or gold, of thorns or flowers, that would never have bound you, but for the formation of the first link on one memorable day. (101)

The seriousness of the tone, the direct address to us who read it, the didactic message all call attention to this passage. We are reminded, forcefully, of the narrative voice—of Pip telling his own story—and we see, clearly, the purpose of his narration.

The image that Pip chooses for this brief homily comes directly from the text of his child-self's recent experiences, though the child Pip has "forgotten" (108) all about it, under the new influence of Miss Havisham and Estella and all that glitter. A convict with a leg-iron, out on "the misty marshes" (47) is—or should be, it would seem—a long way from the supposedly genteel world of Satis House. But Miss Havisham is a prisoner (even the child Pip knows this) as much as Magwitch was or is; and when Pip narrator writes of "the long chain of iron or gold" he alludes to both Magwitch and Miss Havisham. The "link" formed "one memorable day" doubles. Today, at Satis House, Pip has formed—or thinks he has formed—a "link" with Miss Havisham and Estella; this false link will be rendered true by the end of the novel, through forgiveness and parting friendship. On that other "memorable" day—on that "memorable raw afternoon toward evening," out on the marshes (35)—Pip formed an accidental relationship with Magwitch, by helping him to cut through a "link" of iron chain. And though Pip is ashamed of that link now, when the memory of it is forced upon him, and though he tries to reject it later, in the end that link, too, is proved true: "Please God," Pip says to his convict, "I will be as true to you, as you have been to me!" (457).

Pip narrator's ironic choice of the "chain" metaphor at the end of chapter 9 pulls together a number of linkable motifs into a theme. Joe the blacksmith forges it, articulately, as "ever the best of friends" (78). *Great Expectations* is a novel about relationships; and the self-consciousness of the choice of the "chain" metaphor reminds us that one of the important relationships in this novel is that of Pip narrator to his character self. This is a novel about friendships, and part of Pip character's job is to learn to become friends with himself, so that he can befriend the world. The young Pip has considerable trouble learning to be a friend—and his older self has difficulty liking his obnoxious and unfriendly younger self.

The chapter which follows hard upon Pip narrator's thoughts of that "chain of iron or gold" reintroduces Magwitch and links the iron and gold together. At the beginning of the chapter Pip decides to "make [him]self uncommon" by getting "out of Biddy everything she knew" (101). "Wishing to get on in life," he asks her "if she would impart all her learning to me" (102). What the chapter then turns to, however, is what Biddy doesn't know, and what young Pip can only construe as an impediment to his getting on in life. Through the agency of the strange man who first rubs his own leg the way Magwitch did (104) and then stirs his drink "with a file" (106), Magwitch gives

Pip money—the first installment of his "great expectations." But instead of being elated at receiving it, Pip is horrified by the thought of whence it came. And he climbs into bed thanklessly "thinking . . . of the guilty coarse and common thing it was, to be on secret terms of conspiracy with convicts" (107–8).

Friendship and conspiracy both aside, Pip is more closely related to Magwitch than he is to anyone else in the novel: not because Magwitch is, as he says, Pip's "second father" (337), or because he "owns" Pip (339), but because they are from the beginning prisoners and aliens together. Pip recognizes, as a child, that he and Joe share a "freemasonry as fellow-sufferers" and a "good-natured companionship" (42), though later he will ignore and reject Joe's friendship. Pip learns a great deal about friendship from Herbert Pocket, in London—but Herbert is a young gentleman, who makes it easy for Pip to learn from him. He has immense difficulty understanding his relationship with Magwitch, however, and accepting it as love.

Pip has difficulty with emotions other than his own. He is a "very sensitive" child (92), his older self tells us—but he doesn't understand other people's feelings, or even expect them to have any. He ignores Joe's feelings and assumes that Biddy has none. Perhaps it is appropriate that he falls in love with a young woman who has no heart (376). When he brings Magwitch what he has stolen for him, Magwitch is moved by what he perceives as Pip's goodness. Pip narrator carefully records his child-self's response to the convict's emotion: "Something clicked in his throat, as if he had works in him like a clock, and was going to strike. And he smeared his ragged rough sleeve over his eyes" (50). Not only does Pip not understand that Magwitch is crying; he does not even recognize the sounds and gestures which express emotion.

When we first see little Pip out on the marshes he is "a small bundle of shivers, growing afraid of it all and beginning to cry" (36). Magwitch "shiver[s]" also—Pip thinks he has "got the ague" (50)—and he starts to cry. But the child Pip can't see the parallel. Like Magwitch, he is out on the marshes because he has no place else to go; at home he is "a young offender . . . to be dealt with according to the outraged majesty of the law" (54). The narrator sees—creates, even—these connections as he tells his story.

What happens when the narrative voice treats the central character in this way is called irony. Pip narrator knows things which his character self cannot yet know: things which, known, will let him make sense of his life. To return to my earlier suggestion about the moral argument of most great novels, I would suggest that this kind of irony is the trademark of Jane Austen and of James Joyce. It is not usually a characteristic of Dickens's work, however, even in his other first-person narratives.

The particular significance of the narrative irony in *Great Expectations* comes from its being the result of the first-person narrator's attitude toward his younger self's ignorance. What the younger Pip has to learn, as he grows up, is the idea of relation. His narrator self's organization of his life—of the autobiographical novel—sets this theme for us. The end is not for the younger Pip to assume the critical tone of his older self; that tone, when it appears, derives from Pip narrator's shamed and guilty response to his younger self's ignorance. The end is for the character to grow wise: to learn more about "the identity of things." At the end of the novel Pip narrator will accept his character self, satisfied with their relation, pleased with their identity. The irony then will disappear, and the novel will be whole.

Six

Pip's Education

At the end of chapter 9 Pip doesn't blame himself or anybody else—or even that "memorable day"—for the "formation of the first link" in his chain. His warning to us is a bittersweet one: "Pause you who read this, and think for a moment" (101). Pip's faults are his own, not Miss Havisham's or Estella's or anybody else's. And the links of his chain are his own. And they have not ruined his life.

Before Pip was introduced to Satis House, he knew only the forge; having been to Miss Havisham's he knows more, though he may not yet interpret it correctly or value it rightly. *Great Expectations* is a novel about learning and knowing—and even Pip's relationship with Estella is more one of learning and knowing than it is a relationship of love, perhaps. From the beginning of the first chapter, when Pip the child "found out for certain" "the identity of things" (35), this has been a novel about Pip's education.

Learning isn't easy. The lesson of history is not the ironic one that we can't learn, or that we are condemned to repeat the past; rather, it is that learning is hard—and in our laziness we don't seem to want to be smart. In *Oliver Twist* the poor illiterate waif Oliver marvels, upon entering Mr. Brownlow's study, at the "great number of books as seemed to be written to make the world wiser" (*OT*, 144). Mr. Brownlow, however, isn't wise, though he owns and reads books, and he doesn't accept or value the imagination. Wisdom is not a matter of knowing, as intellection alone; it is rather a matter of feeling what we know: of imagination and sympathetic understanding. And that is what's hard to learn.

Mary Anne Evans, a younger contemporary of Dickens whose novels appeared under the name George Eliot, wrote in her journal that "Feeling is a sort of knowledge," that "What seems eminently wanted is a closer comparison between the knowledge which we call rational

& the experience which we call emotional."[33] On the same subject, she wrote to a friend, "If Art does not enlarge men's sympathies, it does nothing morally."[34] Both of these remarks are pertinent for our study of *Great Expectations* and the theme of education in this novel. First, Pip's early attempts at education are restricted to the learning of "things"—information—and manners; and the more he learns, intellectually, about the things that will "raise" him in "society," the more he forgets of human sympathy. Second, his novel has, as its purpose— overtly so, in remarks like that which concludes chapter 9—our education, and the enlargement of our sympathies through an understanding of Pip's story.

Pip's story is not, finally, a story of chains; it is more importantly a story of freedom, and friendship. Freedom and friendship are the same word, etymologically: they both come into the English language from the same Germanic root, *frei*, which means "to love." The bond that friendship makes, then, frees us: freedom becomes much more clearly a social virtue than we might sometimes try to make it, each of us doing his own thing. Both words tell us that you can't be free by yourself. "Ever the best of friends, Pip" is not Joe's threat to his apprentice; it is his pledge for Pip's freedom. Later, Joe gladly gives up Pip's indentures (those papers that "bind" Pip apprentice to the master blacksmith) because Pip is his friend.

To Pip's surprise, however, his new freedom from the forge and his "great expectations" for the future make him lonely rather than happy: he feels it "very sorrowful and strange," he says, that the "first night of [his] bright fortunes should be the loneliest [he] had ever known" (172). He is sad at the prospect of leaving Joe and the world he knows—but still he wants to leave. It takes Joe, in his natural wisdom, to set this problem straight for Pip, and he does it through reference to the double sense of binding that makes friendship free: "Life," he tells Pip, "is made of ever so many partings welded together" (246).

When we understand what Joe says, we will have understood this novel—and our sympathies will be enlarged. Pip narrator understands it, and what he tells as his story records his struggle toward that understanding.

Pip's first learning, in a formal sense, supposedly takes place at Mr. Wopsle's great-aunt's evening school: "that is to say . . . a ridiculous old woman of limited means and unlimited infirmity . . . used to go to sleep from six to seven every evening, in the society of youth who paid twopence per week each, for the improving opportunity of seeing her do it" (74). Mr. Wopsle's great-aunt also has a granddaughter, Biddy, and with her help Pip sets out upon the hard road of scholarship.

As Pip narrator describes it, this hard road is more remarkable for its impediments and dangers than for milestones marking accomplishments. Learning the alphabet is like struggling in "a bramble-bush," and he is "worried and scratched by every letter"; the numbers are "those thieves, the nine figures, who seemed every evening to do something new to disguise themselves and baffle recognition" (75). The child Pip has already associated himself with Magwitch as a boy "going to rob Mrs. Joe," and thus destined for the Hulks (46), and the narrator has reported Mrs. Joe's treating him as a "young offender . . . to be dealt with according to the outraged majesty of the law" and dressed in clothes that, though not necessarily gray like prisoners' uniforms, are designed "like a kind of Reformatory" to restrain "the free use of [his] limbs" (54). Now the narrator connects his child-self's educational endeavors to Magwitch through the bramble-bush and the thieves: "his" thief, in his difficulties, was "stung by nettles, and torn by briars" (36). Further underlining the connection, Pip narrator reckons the time of his first exhibition of his newly won knowledge by reference to Magwitch's capture: he writes Joe a letter "a full year after our hunt on the marshes" (75). These references to Magwitch have no immediate significance, perhaps, other than to remind us that Pip narrator, at least, hasn't forgotten the incident with his convict— and that we shouldn't either. Eventually, these suggestive cross-references will help to clarify the relationship between Magwitch and Pip, and their identification as friends.

Pip's letter describes his happiness with Joe and his active affection for him: he will teach Joe, he says, and they will both be glad; and when Pip is apprenticed to Joe, "woT larX" (75). Dickens clusters the themes and movements of the novel around this simple but difficult communication. It takes Pip "an hour or two" to write these few sentences to Joe; the labor underlines their significance. What they say, together with the confidence they elicit from Joe in response, mark this evening as the climax of their "ever the best of friends" relationship. But when Mrs. Joe comes home that evening, she brings not only the bullying Pumblechook but the disruptive news that Pip is to "go and play" at Miss Havisham's the next day (82).

Magwitch, Joe, friendship, and an innocent desire for learning stand on the one side of Pip's letter; Miss Havisham, Estella, riches, dissatisfaction, frustration, and a newly avaricious attitude toward education stand on the other. Pumblechook takes Pip to Miss Havisham's, and his conversation along the way consists of "nothing but arithmetic." Pip resents Pumblechook's running sums and ignores his questions when he can. But sums are to the point in this new world, more so than in the simple world of the forge which Pip has left behind. Miss Havisham's house is "Satis House," and Satis, as Estella explains, means "enough." The point is not that Pip calculates the worth of what he sees when he enters Miss Havisham's room, but that he recognizes it as worth, as "rich" and "splendid" (87). And as Pip soon discovers, he doesn't know enough, generally, in this new world. He knows but one game, and he doesn't know that one properly: he "calls the knaves, Jacks" (90). And he blames his mistake on Joe, who has "taught" him wrong (92). At the end of the chapter he has learned that he is "a common labouring boy" with coarse hands and thick boots, who calls picture-cards by the wrong name; and "pondering" these things as he walks home, he laments being "much more ignorant than [he] had considered [him]self last night" (94).

At home, Pip complains to Joe, "I am ignorant and backward. . . . I have learnt next to nothing" (100). The next morning he decides to begin immediately to work against his ignorance and determines "to get out of Biddy everything she knew" (101). He proposes to her that, "wishing to get on in life," he would "be obliged to her if she would impart all her learning" to him (102).

Biddy's knowledge—in terms of book-learning—is scarcely in advance of Pip's own, and he realizes woefully that "it would take time, to become uncommon under these circumstances" (103). Still, he resolves to try and heads for home that evening with "a large old English D"—which he supposes "to be a design for a buckle"—to practice copying.

Just as Pip's letter to Joe, the first proof of his "uncommon" scholarly accomplishment, was followed by his embarrassment at Miss Havisham's for being "ignorant" and "a common labouring boy," so here his resolve to "become uncommon" is thrown back in his face by his "common" past. On his way home he must stop for Joe at the public house, where he encounters the man with the file, who is acquainted with Magwitch. When Pip goes to bed that night, he thinks not of the two pounds he has received, but of "the guilty coarse and common thing it was, to be on secret terms of conspiracy with convicts" (107–8).

Whenever Pip has the chance, he confides to Miss Havisham his twin ambitions to learn and to rise. When she inquires "what I had learnt—what I was going to be?" Pip must admit that he is to be apprenticed to Joe; but in the same breath he "enlarge[s] upon [his] knowing nothing and wanting to know everything, in the hope that she might offer some help toward that desirable end" (123). Miss Havisham doesn't help, however; "she seemed," says Pip, "to prefer my being ignorant" (123). What she does undertake for him is to pay for his being apprenticed—"bound" (132–33)—to Joe.

In a sense Pip's life begins again at this point. Pip narrator is careful to represent this new state of his as the awful product of his "ungracious condition of mind," and to blame no one for it: "How much of [it] may have been my own fault, how much Miss Havisham's, how much my sister's, is now of no moment to me or to any one" (134–35). "The change," he says, "was made in me"—and the unhappiness this change brings almost overwhelms him.

Pip narrator's description of this new beginning may remind us of the opening of the novel:

> I remember that . . . I used to stand about the churchyard on Sunday evenings, when night was falling, comparing my own perspective with the windy marsh view, and making out some likeness between them by thinking how flat and low both were, and how on both there came an unknown way and a dark mist and then the sea. (135)

It certainly reminds the narrator of that first scene; the language and the imagery are too close for it to be otherwise. The significance of a return to that opening derives both from Pip's present unhappiness and from what quickly follows: a convict escapes, again, and Magwitch's leg-iron reappears, to punish Mrs. Joe.

Pip is still trying to learn, still full of his "desire to be wiser" (136). He grows too big to continue his "education" at the evening school, but not until "Biddy had imparted to me everything she knew" (136). In his "hunger for information" (137) he even tries to use Mr. Wopsle as a teacher, but soon gives that up as worthless. He tries now to teach Joe, as he had promised to do as a child; only he is not happy being apprenticed to Joe, and "woT larX" is no longer a part of his vocabulary or his set of values. He wants "to be a gentleman" (154), and when he tries to teach Joe he does so "to make Joe less ignorant and common, that he might be worthy of my society and less open to Estella's reproach" (137).

But Pip can't catch up with Estella through what he learns on his own or with Biddy's help; Estella is learning, too, "educating for a lady" (144) in France. His opportunity to catch up comes when Lawyer Jaggers appears and announces that Pip has "great expectations," and is to be "brought up a gentleman" (165). His expectations include, as an immediate guarantee for his future, funds for his "education" (166). A gentleman can't be educated in a village, however, or while living at a forge, so Pip must go to London: "the sooner you leave here," Jaggers advises him, "the better" (169).

Pip's special education is arranged, and he is eager to be away. But "the first night of [his] bright fortunes" is curiously "the loneliest [he] had ever known" (172), and the next is no better: "the second night of my bright fortunes [was] as lonely and unsatisfactory as the first" (176). Except for what we know from our own experience of ourselves in similar circumstances, we might call young Pip a slow learner for not realizing the reason for his lonely unhappiness. But it is hard to learn what one doesn't want to know—and that is Pip's difficulty here.

Once settled in London, Pip forgets his painful parting from his old world. For the first time in his life he has a friend his own age, and he has "expectations." Herbert Pocket is both Pip's friend and his teacher, though what registers for Pip character as Herbert's teaching is nothing more than a short course in city manners: "in London it is not the custom to put the knife in the mouth" (230); "society as a body does not expect one to be so strictly conscientious in emptying one's glass as to turn it bottom upwards with the rim on one's nose" (204); "my dear Handel . . . a dinner napkin will not go into a tumbler" (204). But Herbert is not just a young man with proper manners and an easy congeniality; for all that he impresses Pip as someone who "would never be very successful or rich" (201), he is a true young gentleman. What Herbert teaches Pip, gently, is the meaning of friendship.

Herbert's father is the professional teacher assigned to Pip in London. It is not clear from the narrative what, if anything, Mr. Pocket proposes to teach Pip or expects him to learn. Since Pip is "not designed for any profession" (220), the "mere rudiments" of an education seem to be all that Mr. Pocket thinks he needs. When Pip narrator speaks of his having "applied [him]self to his education" (226), he fails to mention studying—or learning—anything, though he remembers having "stuck to [his] books" (227).

At the end of his education to be a gentleman, Pip discovers himself "fit for nothing" (357). But this realization is in itself something important for Pip to have come to, as it concludes the charade that he has played of studying to be a gentleman. Pip's realization comes, of course, with the collapse of his dreams and expectations, upon the arrival of Magwitch.

In telling Herbert of his new situation, Pip's most pressing concern is himself, and how he can extricate himself from this terrible and shameful difficulty. Herbert responds by reminding Pip that he has a responsibility to Magwitch: "If you were to renounce this patronage and these favours, I suppose you would do so with some faint hope of one day repaying what you have already had" (357). The responsibility that Herbert argues for, however, is not just pecuniary responsibility:

> And you have, and are bound to have, that tenderness for the life he has risked on your account, that you must save him, if possible, from throwing it away. Then you must get him out of England before you stir a finger to extricate yourself. (359)

Pip has introduced the topic of what he should do about Magwitch's appearance by proposing to "go for a soldier": "And I might have gone, my dear Herbert, but for the prospect of taking counsel with your friendship and affection" (357). This "counsel" of Herbert's is of course much more important to Pip than his advice about knives in the mouth and wine glasses on the nose. It is at once Herbert's counsel and his counsel as a friend that Pip must take.

The Pip who wants to "rise" in life has begun, with that ambition, by learning to disregard his friends. Once Pip determines to rise, he and Joe are no longer the "equals" they had seemed before. Pip forgets his respect for Joe because what Pip respects in his life changes. Whereas on the night before he first went to "play" at Miss Havisham's he felt "conscious" of "looking up to Joe in [his] heart" (80), what the heart looks up to no longer has value for Pip, and he looks up only to the place in "society" toward which he climbs.

Herbert has no expectations, and his "general air" seems to tell young Pip, when first they meet in London, that Herbert "would never be very successful or rich" (201). But despite this severe limitation—or perhaps because, with this limitation, he presents no challenge to Pip—he and Herbert become friends.

Herbert has "not a handsome face," but is "extremely amiable and cheerful." His figure is "a little ungainly," but it looks as if it will "always be light and young." And, most important for our young snob in the making, Herbert is "so communicative" that Pip feels "that reserve on my part would be a bad return unsuited to our years" (201). So Pip and Herbert become friends, and Herbert begins to teach Pip the value of friendship. The first lesson is candor. Before Pip can begin to feel uncomfortable about having been "brought up as a blacksmith" (201) Herbert chooses a new name for him from that lowly past: "We are so harmonious," Herbert says, "and you have been a blacksmith. . . . There's a charming piece of music by Handel, called the Harmonious Blacksmith" (202). And thus Pip becomes Handel, and Herbert's friend.

The resonance in Pip's new name, of course, is the reminder of Joe, whom Pip has left behind. Joe has always been Pip's friend and promises "ever" to be so. But Pip doesn't want Joe's friendship, now that he is a young gentleman. For all that Joe is a model friend—and a model "Man," as Pip narrator insists on calling him (301)—he is not a teacher of any great or special talent. Pip narrator praises Joe's radiant goodness—"It is not possible to know how far the influence of any amiable honest-hearted duty-doing man flies out into the world" (135)—but that goodness can't teach Pip contentment at the forge, or make him less "ashamed of home" (134). Joe's goodness may have "touched [Pip's] self in going by," but as long as Pip is at the forge, he still works unhappily "against the grain" (135). Joe's friendship—and the promise of larks—can't teach Pip happiness.

Joe's friendship, however, never deserts Pip. "Ever the best of friends" is Joe's promise, and nothing Pip can do will change that, as far as Joe is concerned. When Pip awakens from his delirium, late in the novel, Joe is beside him. Joe is there because he is needed. And laying his head beside Pip's on the pillow, he says, "you and me was ever friends. And when you're well enough to go out for a ride—what larks!" (472).

When Pip and Joe have gone on their ride—Pip with his head on

Joe's shoulder (476)—Joe leaves. His friendship will not impose on Pip's freedom, and Pip is "well enough" to be without him. "Ever the best of friends," is the message he leaves (481).

That Pip follows Joe, this time, back to the forge proves that Pip has learned something. Before, Pip would have been content to use Joe's help, let him go, and send a barrel of oysters as a thank you. But Pip has no money now, and no expectations except those that he creates out of his own heart.

In his open relationship with Herbert, Pip learns what friendship is. Seeing his younger self with Herbert, Pip narrator says, "I had never felt before what it is to have a friend" (356). Eventually, after Magwitch's capture, Herbert finds it necessary to absent himself from London for a time. "I am very much afraid I must go," he tells Pip, "when you need me most." Pip's answer is clear, and sure: "Herbert, I shall always need you, because I shall always love you; but my need is no greater now, than at another time" (459).

It takes Pip a long time to learn affection. Perhaps this is because he grew up an unwanted child, scourged by Tickler and the "moral goads" (57) of his piously unfeeling elders. Whatever the cause—and again, Pip narrator doesn't try to allocate or assign blame—the painful fact remains that it takes Pip a long, hard time to learn the selflessness which lets him love. Learning "things" sometimes seems to be a better protection against a hostile world than learning affection, and the young Pip is victimized for a long time by this seeming. His best teacher for the difficult lesson of selflessness and love is Herbert. This may be because, being the same age, he and Pip are able to be free and open with each other. It may be because Pip, secure for the moment in his expectations, is for the first time able to think and act generously, and to learn for himself what generosity is. Again, whatever the reason, Pip does learn friendship with Herbert, and learns with him the value of friendship. The most harmonious music in the whole novel is that played by Herbert with his hands in Handel's, on his return from France: "Handel, my dear fellow, how are you, and again how are you, and again how are you?" (354). Pip narrator's memory of those words is like the song which the narrator of *Our Mutual Friend* repeats toward the end of that next Dickens novel: "O 'tis love, 'tis love, 'tis love, that makes the world go round!" (*OMF,* 739).

Pip's first chance to practice what he has learned comes with Magwitch's capture. His pledge—"Please God, I will be as true to you, as you have been to me!" (457)—is its test. It rings back through the novel, to that first "memorable" day, with which all this began.

Seven

Pip's Education, Continued

Not all of Pip's lessons are lessons in affection and generosity such as Herbert teaches him, or Joe offers him by his noble example. We have discussed what Pip learns at Satis House of the desirability of what is "rich" and "splendid"; what Pip learns in Little Britain from the well-intentioned Wemmick is not much different, and the lesson of his guardian's example in dealing with life is—in the abstract, at least—not at all unlike Miss Havisham's.

Pip should be suspicious of Wemmick from the very beginning of their acquaintance: when upon leaving the office, Pip puts out his hand, "Mr. Wemmick at first looked at it as if he thought I wanted something." Then Wemmick corrects himself and says to Pip, "To be sure! Yes. You're in the habit of shaking hands?" (197).

Wemmick doesn't shake hands, as a rule: there's nothing to be gained by such a gesture. And Wemmick's philosophy is one of gain; his "guiding star" is "Get hold of portable property" (224). Such, at any rate, is his public or business philosophy; but "the office is one thing, and private life is another" (221), according to Wemmick, and he purports to conduct his life in Little Britain quite differently from his life at Walworth. At the Castle he is affectionate and gentle, "shaking hands" with his Aged Parent (230) and "stealing his arm around Miss Skiffins's waist" (316). Such conduct is possible for him at Walworth, presumably because the Castle is separated from the rest of the world by a four-foot moat with a plank for a drawbridge: "I hoist it up," Wemmick says, "and cut off the communication" (229). But though Wemmick claims to separate his hard-faced office life from his softened, human life at home, the treasures of the Castle, awkwardly, are bits of "portable property" bequeathed him by his business associates at Newgate.

When Pip mentions to Wemmick that he is "desirous to serve a friend," Wemmick responds "as if his opinion were dead against any fatal weakness of that sort" (309). To Wemmick, serving a friend is a waste of "portable property": one might as well "pitch [his] money into the Thames." Should a man "invest portable property in a friend?" he asks, rhetorically; and he answers, with emphasis, "Certainly he should not" (310).

But that opinion is Wemmick's Little Britain opinion, and presumably, according to the fiction Wemmick has created for himself, his "Walworth sentiments" will be different (310). When, at the Castle, Pip has made a full representation of his plan for helping Herbert, Wemmick agrees to aid him. His initial response, however, even at Walworth, is skeptical and defensive:

> Wemmick was silent for a little while, and then said with a kind of start, "Well you know, Mr. Pip, I must tell you one thing. This is devilish good of you."
>
> "Say you'll help me to be good then," said I.
>
> "Ecod," replied Wemmick, shaking his head, "that's not my trade." (314)

When Wemmick goes out of his way to warn Pip of Magwitch's being watched, he does so from the Castle. But his thinking is Little Britain thinking, still. At the conclusion of his advice, and in such a friendly Walworth manner that he lets Pip shake his hands and then lays his hands upon Pip's shoulders, Wemmick whispers solemnly, "Avail yourself . . . of his portable property. You don't know what may happen to him. Don't let anything happen to the portable property" (386).

Weemick's double life is a sham—just as the Castle is. A sentimentally benign interpretation of his character would have him comically schizophrenic, living one life at the office and another at home. That would be bad enough, for Dickens, and a serious lesson for us. But Wemmick is not a model schizophrenic; he is much worse. A close examination of his values makes it clear that Little Britain and Walworth are one world, and in both places the values taught, the lessons offered, are self-defense and portable property. "Every man's business," he says, "is portable property" (421).

At the office Wemmick shuts off his humanity, in order to do his worldly business. At the Castle he shuts out the world—"I cut off the communication," he says, revealingly—and presumes to be human. Pip is almost taken in by this pretense, as a young man. But "you can't shut out the world," Dickens says; "you are in it, to be of it." And as for business, and "portable property": we all have an obligation to the world—to "make the best of it"—not just to ourselves. The world, for Dickens, is human business. The proper businessman must learn to love it.

Wemmick has a very limited understanding of the possibilities of human existence; the Aged's notion that "this pretty pleasure-ground . . . and these beautiful works upon it ought to be kept together by the Nation . . . for the people's enjoyment" (230) is a wonderfully ironic and comic response to his son's social conscience. Still, Wemmick is innocent—naive—in his defensiveness, and even generously well-meaning in his acts and advices. Lawyer Jaggers, however, is a sinister and intellectually selfish man. And though he offers his act of "saving" Estella (425) as in some way a justification for his life, that act is the only generously good deed he ever performs. Even this good deed is corrupted by his refusal to involve himself—despite what he must know—in what becomes of Estella as Miss Havisham's ward or adopted daughter.

Jaggers would contest my saying that he "must know." The key to Jaggers's self-defense lies in his refusal to know anything that might involve or incriminate him: and he thinks of involvement in this crazy, dangerous world as though it is necessarily incriminating. Though he has no locks upon his doors, he keeps the world away from him as effectively as Miss Havisham does, with her barred and shuttered windows.[35] Miss Havisham knows the meaning of her shutting out of life—knows that, in the end, she will herself replace the rotted wedding cake upon the bride's table (117)—and she hates it. Jaggers tries to survive by means of his retreat, pretending that his defense against the world is life.

Early in the novel Pip almost makes the mistake of telling Miss Havisham what day it is. She interrupts him: "There, there! I know nothing of the days of the week, I know nothing of the weeks of the year" (91). When Pip returns he says "Today is—" and again she interrupts him: "I don't want to know," she says, impatiently (112).

In Dickens's world, not to know is dangerous; not to want to know is always wrong. For Miss Havisham, "I don't want to know" is supposedly self-defense. But though her intentional isolation from the living, changing world—her refusal to "know" it any more—may have begun as a hurt creature's self-defense, it becomes her destroyer. Determinedly ignorant of the world, she cuts herself off from everything except her festering hatred for men and her self-pity. Her original ambition for Estella, she says, was "to save her from misery like mine" (415); but isolated from the world and utterly alienated in her defensiveness, she perverts even this one attempt at human responsibility.

Lawyer Jaggers seems to be quite a different creature. His windows aren't barred—he has no locks on his doors at all—and he walks freely about in the world, secure in his knowledge of it. When he appears in The Three Jolly Bargemen, he badgers the men there with his knowledge. What he claims—parades, enforces—is knowledge not of facts but of character. Mr. Wopsle makes the mistake of supposing on the basis of what he has read in a newspaper that a man being tried for murder must be guilty. Jaggers probes—"Guilty, of course?"—and Wopsle commits himself: "I do say Guilty." Jaggers responds, "I know you do . . . I knew you would." He continues, then: "Do you know, or do you not know, that the law of England supposes every man to be innocent until he is proved—proved to be guilty? . . . Either you know it, or you don't know it. . . . Do you know it, or don't you know it. . . . Certainly you know it" (161). Jaggers's manner, says the narrator, seems to express his "knowing something secret about every one of us" (163).

But we must not be taken in by Jaggers's knowing so much. He knows what he can make use of, and is careful not to know what might work against him. He values knowledge only for its usefulness to himself, and for the power derivable from such useful knowledge.

When approached by his clients, in London, he immediately says to them, "I want to know no more than I know" (191). When Pip tries to speak about Magwitch, Jaggers stops him: "Don't tell me anything; I don't want to know anything; I am not curious" (340). He prides himself on having "adhered to the strict line of fact," on never having made "the least departure from the strict line of fact" (351) in his relationship with Pip.

Like Miss Havisham, Jaggers has known all along that Pip misleads himself as to the source of his fortune—and like Miss Havisham, Jaggers lets Pip continue in his error. Miss Havisham's fostering of Pip's ignorance, his misconception, is understandable though still perverse; the situation merely gives her an opportunity to hurt a male, to enact her pitiful revenge. Jaggers, however, has no reason for wanting Pip to make such an awkward and destructive mistake. His carefully irresponsible complicity in Pip's error is purely perverse. Jaggers is much worse, morally, than Miss Havisham; and whereas at the end of the novel Pip forgives a repentant Miss Havisham, the last he shows us of Jaggers—and Wemmick—they are doing, together, what they have always done.

Jaggers is worse than Miss Havisham because his motivation is so meanly selfish. Jaggers has not been hurt by the world or by any particular falseness practiced upon him. He has never made the mistake of loving someone. Rather, he sees the "evil" of the world (424), and determines not to be hurt by it. As his defense he chooses control: he has no qualms about committing wrong himself if wrongdoing and injustice will keep him in control of the world around him. Control becomes a passion for Jaggers—his only passion—and an obsession. His pleasure in Pip's error about the identity of his benefactor is the obsessive response of a passionately selfish man.

When Pip presents himself at Jaggers's office with the knowledge of who his benefactor is, Jaggers refuses to let Pip "tell" him anything—"I don't want to know anything; I am not curious" (350)—and then refuses to apologize for or to try to excuse or even to acknowledge his participation in Pip's error: "I am not at all responsible for that," he says (350). When he insists that he has "always adhered to the strict line of fact" (351), he makes, implicitly, a careful distinction between fact and truth. As far as Jaggers "knows," factually and professionally, Magwitch is in Australia; what he knows, in truth—that Magwitch is actually in London—is not to be discussed. Jaggers protects himself; that is his profession, his business. He will not let himself become involved in anyone else's life.

When Pip returns to Little Britain, later, with his knowledge of who Magwitch is, he catches Jaggers off his guard by knowing something more than Jaggers knows. Knowledge, for Jaggers, is a weapon: its only function is self-defense. When Pip knows something he doesn't know, Jaggers is in a dangerous situation.

Before he can talk with Jaggers about Magwitch, Pip has business to transact with him. Pip has authority from Miss Havisham to draw nine hundred pounds from her account, for Herbert. "I am sorry, Pip," says Jaggers, "that we do nothing for *you*." Pip responds that Miss Havisham offered to assist him, but that he declined her offer. "Every man should know his own business," Jaggers replies, and then repeats the observation: "I should *not* have told her No, if I had been you . . . but every man ought to know his own business best" (421).

Knowing one's own business best is in a sense—a perverse, twisted sense—Jaggers's motto. When Pip tells him that Miss Havisham has given him what information she had about Estella, Jaggers responds: "I don't think I should have done so, if I had been Miss Havisham. But *she* ought to know her own business best" (421). Knowledge, for Jaggers, is not something to be given away; it is to Jaggers what "portable property" is to Wemmick. Just as Wemmick says, acquisitively, "Every man's business . . . is portable property" (421), so Jaggers might say, with obsessive defensiveness, "Every man's business is controlling knowledge."

But Pip knows more than Jaggers knows, this time: "I know more of the history of Miss Havisham's adopted child," he says, "than Miss Havisham herself does, sir. I know her mother." Jaggers knows Estella's mother; it is Molly: but he has not previously known that Pip knows this. His response is defensive, noncommittal: "Yes? . . . Yes?" Then Pip presses his advantage: a defensive, determinedly uninvolved, unresponsive man who thinks only in adversarial terms has to be challenged and pursued. "Perhaps I know more of Estella's history than even you do," Pip says; "I know her father too" (422).

Pip has come to Jaggers, not to use his knowledge to gain some advantage for himself or to abuse Jaggers with it. Pip simply presents his knowledge as his knowledge, and asks Jaggers to complete it, to verify if he can the conclusions Pip has drawn from what he knows. Jaggers's first response is to ignore Pip and return to his "business": "Hah! . . . What item was it you were at, Wemmick, when Mr. Pip came in?" (423).

Pip insists, and finally persuades Jaggers to tell him what he knows. Jaggers "put[s] the case"—with the strict qualification, "Mind! I admit nothing" (424)—in his most defensive manner. Telling what he knows is an ordeal for Jaggers, and instead of simply giving Pip information, he "put[s] the case" as though he were on trial. When he has submitted his evidence, he returns to his business with the same words he had used before: "Now, Wemmick . . . what item was it you were at, when Mr. Pip came in?" (426).

What was almost human in Jaggers, as he "put the case," is closed off again. When a poor thief who "seemed to be always in trouble" enters the office "to announce that his eldest daughter [has been] taken up on suspicion of shop-lifting" (426) and makes the mistake of shedding "a tear," Jaggers resumes his usual manner, triumphantly: "Get out of this office," he says; "I'll have no feelings here. Get out" (427).

Great Expectations is a novel about Pip's education, and the end or goal of his education is that freedom which is friendship. Jaggers is not free because he cannot comprehend friendship. He is locked into his own defensiveness. He lives by power and control, and does not trust affection. There is no evidence in the novel that Jaggers, like Miss Havisham, has had his affection tricked or abused. He has not been brutalized or otherwise victimized by treachery; there is nothing, thus, to excuse or extenuate his cruelty. Therefore, though Miss Havisham is forgiven, before her death, Jaggers is sent back to his psychologically and symbolically solitary cell. His example—the lesson that he would teach—is rejected.

When Pip goes to Satis House upon learning the identity of his real benefactor, he begins by blaming Miss Havisham for his condition: "I am as unhappy as you can ever have meant me to be," he says. His purpose in speaking to her is not to complain, but that is what he does:

> "But when I fell into the mistake I have so long remained in, at least you led me on?" said I.
> "Yes," she returned . . . "I let you go on."
> "Was that kind?"
> "Who am I . . . who am I, for God's sake, that I should be kind?" (373)

Pip apologizes for this "weak complaint," and she reminds him, cruelly, of the ultimate source of his errors: "You made your own snares" (374).

The Pip who has been so mistaken, and whose mistakes have led him into shameful unkindness, comes to Miss Havisham seeking kindness. The kindness that he seeks, however, is not for himself but for Herbert. She ignores his request when he makes it, but thereafter sends word that he is to come to see her on "a matter of business" (403). His first sense when he sees her this time is that there is "an air of utter loneliness upon her," and he is moved to "pity" her. He stands "compassionating" her as they speak. Miss Havisham, too, is pitying, now, and contrite: "I am not all stone," she says; "But perhaps you can never believe, now, that there is anything human in my heart?" (408). Pip reassures her, and she continues "in an unwonted tone of sympathy" (409). Their mutual sympathy is appropriate; it is something that they both have had to learn, through suffering.

As Pip watches Miss Havisham in her distress, the narrator reviews what Pip "knew," standing there: and though what he "knew" was that she had done wrong, he also "knew," he says, "compassion" for her (411). Miss Havisham, in her turn, explains to him that she "did not know what [she] had done" until she "saw in [Pip] a looking glass that showed [her] what [she] once felt" (411). As his suffering reminds her of her own, it teaches her both remorse and pity. She speaks, he says, with "an earnest womanly compassion" and with "new affection" for him, as she tells the sordid story of how with her "teachings" and her "lessons" she "stole [Estella's] heart away, and put ice in its place" (412). "If you knew all my story," she concludes, burdened now with guilt, "you would have some compassion for me" (412).

Pip does have pity on Miss Havisham and forgives her. He has learned compassion and affection well enough by now to free Miss Havisham—or to try to, at any rate: she dies repentant, knowing that she has done wrong, saying over and over, "What have I done?" and "When she first came, I meant to save her from misery like mine," and "Take the pencil and write under my name, 'I forgive her!' " (415).

Estella is not saved from misery, of course. Miss Havisham's "teachings" and "lessons" make Estella both miserable herself and the agency for inflicting misery on others. Estella knows her own misery early on, even before she marries Drummle: she is "tired of [her]self" (322) and "tired of the life [she has] led" (377). She does not "comprehend" love as an emotion because her "lessons" have taught her to feel nothing, to be "cold" (322). When Miss Havisham complains that Estella has no affection even for her "mother by adoption," Estella answers with reference to what she has been taught: she has sat as a child, she tells Miss Havisham, "learning your lessons," and has never been "unmindful of your lessons." "Who taught me to be proud?" she asks; "Who praised me when I learned my lesson?" And again: "Who taught me to be hard? . . . Who praised me when I had learned my lesson?" (323). What Miss Havisham has "taught" Estella has made her what she is, she insists (324); the kindest thing she can do, having been so taught, so "formed," is warn Pip away from her (376).

At the end of the novel Estella is changed. She, too, can "understand" now, what feelings and affections are: what the "heart" is. She has been "taught," she says, by "suffering," which "has been stronger than all other teaching" (493). When Dickens rewrote the ending of the novel, this notion is the only thing he saved from the first version. In the original ending Pip narrator says: "in her voice, and in her touch, [Estella] gave me the assurance, that suffering had been stronger than Miss Havisham's teaching, and had given her a heart to understand what my heart used to be."[36] Her education is not unlike Miss Havisham's, or Pip's. They all learn through suffering: and what they learn is affection, compassion, friendship.

What Estella learns, having been "bent, broken, but . . . into a better shape" (453), is how to be "friends." Like Miss Havisham, she asks Pip to "forgive" her (493)—just as Pip asks Joe and Biddy to "forgive" him (488). And then she asks Pip to assure her that they are "friends." That they are friends—"and will continue friends apart" (493)—is the conclusion of the novel.

The real lesson of *Great Expectations* is friendship. Joe has difficulty learning to read and write; he is, by his own admission "so awful dull" (174). But Joe knows what friendship is, and what it means. Affection and sympathy make him "ever the best of friends"—and Joe knows, has "calc'lated," that friendship "lead[s] to larks" (128).

In every Dickens novel except *The Mystery of Edwin Drood*, part of the conclusion involves various good young people getting married, and usually having children. With the exception of Mr. Pickwick, who is an old man at the beginning of his novel and a "retired" old man at the end, and Oliver Twist, who is retired by Dickens at the end of his novel at the ripe old age of eleven, the central character of every Dickens novel up to *A Tale of Two Cities* marries at the end. This marriage generally indicates, in part, the achievement of the central character's growing up, or education; it also signifies Dickens's hope for the future.

At the end of *Little Dorrit*, when Amy Dorrit and Arthur Clennam are married, they "paused for a moment . . . in the autumn morning sun's bright rays, and then went down." The rhetoric of the concluding paragraph of that novel is brilliant—more so, perhaps, than even the sun's bright rays shining on this real world. When Amy and Arthur "went down," they "went down into a modest life of usefulness and happiness"; they "went down" to take care of their children and Amy's sister's poor, neglected children; they "went down" to take care of Amy's worthless brother, too. "They went down," the narrator tells us, to conclude the novel, "into the roaring streets, inseparable and blessed; and as they passed along in sunshine and shade, the noisy and the eager, and the arrogant and the froward and the vain, fretted and chafed, and made their usual uproar" (*LD*, 894–95). The hope that Dickens expresses here does not change the world directly, or begin it over with a new generation of goodness. Rather, it works *in* the world that exists.

Beginning with *A Tale of Two Cities*, Dickens's central characters don't marry at the ends of their novels. Rather, they learn friendship, and the freedom that friendship means. Joe Gargery articulates the idea best, in *Great Expectations*: "Life," he tells Pip, "is made of ever so many partings welded together" (246). Joe may not be a "scholar" (100), but he is a wise man. And though he is not Pip's most accomplished teacher, he is certainly the best example in the novel of a wise—and educated—man. He and Herbert teach Pip friendship, and the value of friendship. Estella learns its value, too—in part through Pip. In the end, though Estella and Pip do not marry—they "will continue friends apart," Estella says (493)—Joe is the best man, and Pip goes off to make his family with Herbert and Clara and do his business in this world.

Pip learns friendship, and friendship earns him the freedom to love Estella, even though they are apart. Because Pip learns this, and in learning it grows wise, his life is not ruined. Indeed, we can expect— from the book he has written, and what it tells us—that his life will have a happy ending.

And as Pip wrote this book for us, may our lives—we "who read this" (101)—have such happy endings also.

Eight

Magwitch

When the time comes for Magwitch to tell Pip and Herbert his story, he tells it in idioms and phrases that should remind us of Pip's story. The reminders aren't all direct or straight, however; some of them are ironic, some but echoes that make associations possible. These connections between Magwitch's and Pip's stories are important, both for Pip narrator and for us. Magwitch dreams himself into a relationship with Pip—becomes, as he sees it, Pip's "second father"—and proposes to live vicariously through the boy he has "made a gentleman on" (337). As Pip narrator tells his own story—which includes Magwitch and his story, of course—the details he chooses to emphasize and the language he uses to create his life's sense represent the relationship he sees between himself and Magwitch. From his childhood on Pip thinks of Magwitch as "my convict"; and every echo, every suggestive association serves to forge more securely the connection between them.

Magwitch tells his story in two parts: his childhood and early life, up through his partnership with Compeyson, make up the first part, his life in Australia the second. In the second part—which he tells first, to Pip alone—as he herded sheep, living "in a solitary hut, not seeing no faces but the faces of sheep," Magwitch kept Pip's face constantly before his mind's eye: "I see you there a many times," he says, "as plain as ever I see you on them misty marshes" (337). He promised himself then—or rather he promised his God: Magwitch believes in "the Almighty" (467), and swears by him and upon his book, or "under the open heavens" (337)—to live his life for Pip. When he got his liberty, he says, and "went for [him]self," he "went for" Pip: "In every single thing I went for, I went for you" (339).

The first part of his life, as Magwitch tells it, covers the time from his "becom[ing] aware of [him]self" as a child down to his meeting with Pip out on the marshes. The beginnings of Magwitch's story are not related to Pip's life—except as Pip narrator makes them so, by forming his recollection of his own childhood in language that matches Magwitch's representation of his.

This segment of Magwitch's life includes the story of his becoming Compeyson's "pardner" (362), which has no connection with Pip as far as Magwitch knows; Pip discovers his relationship to that part of his convict's life only through Herbert's knowledge that the Arthur who was "in with Compeyson" (363) was Arthur Havisham, and that Compeyson himself was "the man who professed to be Miss Havisham's lover (367). The conclusion of the Compeyson incident comes with Magwitch's escape from the Hulks: "I escaped to the shore, and was hiding among the graves there, envying them as was in 'em and all over, when I first see my boy" (366). It takes him but three short paragraphs to cover what Pip doesn't know from his own experience about Magwitch's life between then and now. "By my boy," he says, "I was giv to understand as Compeyson was out on them marshes too" (366). He captures Compeyson, and is captured himself. Compeyson's "punishment was light," he notes, whereas he was "sent for life." He concludes, then, in an evidentiary way: "I didn't stop for life . . . being here" (366).

The meaning of Magwitch's story, for Magwitch, is that it concludes with his being with his boy, the boy who "stood [his] friend" out there on the marshes fifteen years before.

The meaning of Magwitch's story for Pip is more complicated. We have talked about friendship, and about education, and about the end of education being friendship. I want now to discuss those same themes again, with the focus on Magwitch, and at the same time to keep track of Pip narrator's carefully continuous weaving of himself into Magwitch's life. We have talked about Pip's relationships with Joe and Herbert, and we will talk about his relationship with Estella. But for many readers Pip's relationship with Magwitch is the most important one, thematically. Pip's relationships with Herbert and Joe and even Estella continue beyond the novel; they are "friends" at the end, and "will continue" so. Pip's relationship with Magwitch, however, is resolved—completed—by Magwitch's death.

The story that Magwitch tells to Pip and Herbert in chapter 42 is told almost without interruption. His first version of it is very short: "short and handy," he says, "put . . . into a mouthful of English. In jail and out of jail, in jail and out of jail, in jail and out of jail. There, you've got it." In his life before he "got shipped off" to Australia Magwitch finds but one incident worth any sort of particular mention: that "Pip stood [his] friend" (360).

Following this brief résumé, Magwitch tells his "story" in greater detail; and as he tells it, it echoes Pip's own story as he told it to us in chapter 1. Recalling for us Pip's "My first most broad and vivid impression of the identity of things" (35), Magwitch says, "I first become aware of myself, down in Essex, a thieving turnips for a living." As Pip's first awareness ends with his seeing himself "a small bundle of shivers" (36), Magwitch ends: "Summun had run away from me— a man—a tinker—and he'd took the fire with him, and left me wery cold" (360).

Philip Pirrip knows his name, but has "called himself Pip" (35). His convict "know'd [his] name to be Magwitch, christn'd Abel" (360). Just as Pip recalled himself as being "undersized for his years, and not strong" (36), Magwitch remembers his small self having "as little on him as in him" (361). Pip remarks his having been "brought up by hand" at the forge (39); Magwitch, never "brought up" at all—except "to be a warmint" (345), speaks of being "took up" instead: "I was took up, took up, took up to that extent that I reg'larly grow'd up took up" (361).

When Pip first saw Magwitch out on the marshes he was "a man who had been soaked in water, and smothered in mud, and lamed by stones, and cut by flints, and stung by nettles, and torn by briars" (36). In his own narration Magwitch generalizes all of this briefly: "I've been done everything to, pretty well—except hanged" (360).

Magwitch's education has been slight, and simple: "A deserting soldier in a Traveller's Rest . . . learnt me to read; and a travelling Giant what signed his name at a penny a time learnt me to write." His career has been one of "tramping, begging, thieving, working sometimes when [he] could"; and through being "a bit of a poacher, a bit of a labourer, a bit of a waggoner, a bit of a haymaker, a bit of a hawker, a bit of most things that don't pay and lead to trouble," he says, "I got to be a man" (361).

From "thieving turnips for a living" on, Magwitch has done what he has done to stay alive: "I must put something into my stomach, mustn't I?" (361). As Magwitch tells his story, he justifies to himself his small crimes, using the same reason that Joe used when Magwitch was taken up by the soldiers out on the marshes: "we wouldn't have you starved to death . . . poor miserable fellow-creatur" (71). Stealing—or maybe almost anything else—to keep from being "starved to death" is not really a crime, as Magwitch sees it.

Magwitch's real criminal career began, he says, when he met Compeyson. Significantly, the first things he tells Pip and Herbert about Compeyson are that "he set up fur a gentleman," and that "he'd been to a public boarding-school and had learning" (361). When, after four or five years of swindling, he and Compeyson are finally arrested and brought to trial—"separate defenses," Compeyson insists—part of the distinction made between them in court is that whereas Compeyson is "well brought up," Magwitch is "ill brought up"; and "when it come to character," Magwitch recalls, "warn't it Compeyson as had been to the school" and can make advantage for himself from that. Compeyson argues eloquently and dramatically in his own defense, "wi' verses in his speech, too"; Magwitch can only say, "Gentlemen, this man at my side is a most precious rascal" (365).

The issue here, for Dickens and for Pip narrator, is Magwitch's character. Magwitch tells Pip that, even as a child, he "got the name of being hardened" (361), and he is hardened, according to the story he tells, by his rough life. But his story also carries the extenuating explanation of his being hardened by that life. As Magwitch explains himself he doesn't blame the world for his woes; he asserts with some passion his need to "eat and drink" (362) in order to stay alive, but notes almost objectively our complaint—or that of our peers—at his giving in to that biological necessity in such antisocial ways.

When Magwitch appears to Pip out on the marshes in chapter 1 as a "fearful man" with a "terrible voice" (36), what he wants most, as usual, is food. He eats the bread he finds in Pip's pocket "ravenously" and threatens to eat his "fat cheeks" (36) as well. When he presses Pip to bring him "wittles" and a "file," he concludes with this warning: "You fail . . . and your heart and your liver shall be tore out, roasted, and ate" (38).

When Pip returns in chapter 3 with food and a file for this hungry, chained man he changes Magwitch's life. When Magwitch refers later to Pip's having "stood [his] friend" (362) he is referring to this scene, of course. It is not Pip's giving Magwitch the file that changes his life, though the file enables him to free himself from his leg-iron. Nor is it simply the food that changes his life: food is food, and Magwitch eats it like a "dog" (50). What changes Magwitch's life is the idea of friendship, which gives his life meaning: and meaning is more important than either animal sustenance or physical freedom.

Without intending to do so, but in the simple innocence of childhood, Pip begins a conversation with Magwitch. Though he sees Magwitch eating like Joe's dog, Pip treats him like a human—like a friend. "I think you have got the ague," he observes, sympathetically; "It's bad about here. . . . You've been lying out on the meshes, and they're dreadful aguish" (50). When Magwitch hears a noise, his immediate response is not to distrust Pip, as having betrayed him, but to beg him not to have done so: "You're not a deceiving imp? You brought no one with you?" (50). The form of his questions—he doesn't say "Are you a deceiving imp? Did you bring anybody with you"—suggests that Magwitch wants not to be betrayed, not so much because he doesn't want to be taken as because he wants this boy to be kind to him. Magwitch doesn't stop to think that Pip may have come to him out of terror, afraid of the consequences of not coming; he is moved by Pip's being there this Christmas morning, and his emotion creates the meaning of the scene.

Though Magwitch is "gobbling mincemeat, meat bone, bread, cheese, and pork pie, all at once," and "staring distrustfully while he did so at the mists all round us"—though he eats like a dog, taking "strong sharp sudden bites" (50) and "look[ing] sideways here and there . . . as if he thought there was danger in every direction" (51)—

this meal out on the marshes is much more significant as a meal than the awful and uncomfortable Christmas dinner Pip will have at the forge later this same day. Without Pip's or Magwitch's intending it to be so, this meal has become, in Magwitch's eyes, an act of companionship—the word means "bread-sharing," etymologically—and it will be remembered by him as such.

When Pip has assured Magwitch that he has not betrayed him, Magwitch says:

> "Well . . . I believe you. You'd be but a fierce young hound indeed, if at your time of life you could help to hunt a wretched warmint, hunted as near death and dunghill as this poor wretched warmint is."
>
> Something clicked in his throat, as if he had works in him like a clock, and was going to strike. And he smeared his ragged rough sleeve over his eyes.
>
> Pitying his desolation, and watching him as he gradually settled down upon the pie, I made bold to say, "I am glad you enjoy it."
>
> "Did you speak?"
>
> "I said I was glad you enjoyed it."
>
> "Thankee, my boy. I do." (50)

The scene is whole. And though Pip doesn't understand what it means to Magwitch—he doesn't recognize the "something [that] clicked in his throat" as emotion, or that when "he smeared his ragged rough sleeve over his eyes" it was to dry them—Pip is moved to pity him. Pip's "pitying his desolation" civilizes Magwitch, gives him manners even: "Thankee, my boy. I do."

Everything good in Magwitch's life follows from this meeting with Pip on the marshes, and from Pip's friendly conversation with him for this brief moment. He never forgets it. It becomes for him symbolic of what *human* life, which he has never experienced, might be.

Pip narrator's memory of his torment at home on Christmas eve, prior to his theft, is loaded with images which connect his child self with Magwitch and tell us that he understands Magwitch's place in his own life. Pip the child can't comprehend, certainly, a relationship between himself and Magwitch; the coincidences that he sees simply remind him of what he is about to do. For Pip narrator, however, who knows both that relationship and its immense significance, these otherwise ironic coincidences become part of the fabric of his recollective understanding.

When Pip the child stirs the pudding that Christmas Eve, he has the piece of bread and butter saved from his tea in his trouser-leg. He tries stirring the pudding "with the load upon [his] leg," but that reminds him "of the man with the load on *his* leg" (45). When he asks one too many questions—"I wonder who's put into prison ships, and why they're put there?"—Mrs. Joe responds, furiously, "People are put in the Hulks because they murder, and because they rob, and forge, and do all sorts of bad; and they always begin by asking questions." Pip's questions are all about his convict, and what his escape means; the answers he gets tell him that, like his convict, he belongs on a prison ship: "I felt fearfully sensible of the great convenience that the Hulks were handy for me. I was clearly on my way there. I had begun by asking questions, and I was going to rob Mrs. Joe" (46). Finally, as he runs out across the marshes the next morning, with the stolen food and the file, Pip finds that he can't warm his feet because "the damp cold seemed riveted" to them, "as the iron was riveted to the leg of the man I was running hard to meet" (48).

These coincidences don't signify to the child Pip any sort of relationship between himself and Magwitch; they are simply ironic—and disturbing. The closest Pip the child comes to thinking of himself and Magwitch as related is in his calling him, in his child's mind, "my convict." To Pip narrator, however, these matchings and parallels are directly significant; and he insists that we notice them, and notice the relationship they create. Pip narrator insists that we pay close attention to Magwitch at this early point in the novel because he knows how important Magwitch becomes later on. The first level of reading in these opening chapters tells us that Pip is important to Magwitch; the second tells us that Magwitch is important to Pip.

As the child Pip runs out across the marshes on Christmas morning, with the cold "riveted" to his feet "as the iron was riveted to the leg" of Magwitch, Pip narrator intrudes with a seemingly irrelevant bit of information: "I knew my way to the Battery, pretty straight, for I had been down there on a Sunday with Joe, and Joe, sitting on an old gun, had told me that when I was 'prentice to him regularly bound, we would have such Larks there!" (48). This digression—as it seems—distracts us from our focus on Pip's running through the mists, looking for Magwitch. It breaks the dramatic effect, interferes with our expectations. But if our attention is all on the child Pip's adventures on the marshes, we are misreading, I think: running with the plot, we are missing the meaning. Part of Dickens's brilliance is that while he writes dramatically entertaining adventure stories, his works are also seriously moral and thoughtful novels. At the serious level, there are rarely any digressions in a Dickens novel: everything focuses, if we read well enough.

When Pip narrator tells us about that Sunday visit to the old Battery with Joe, and Joe's saying "that when I was 'prentice to him regularly bound, we would have such Larks there!" he is superimposing the great expectation of "Larks"—of happiness—upon his relationship with Magwitch. This is the first mention of "Larks" in the novel, the first reference to Joe's special, coded formulation of what happiness is. Its introduction here, at this point, in the midst of this scene, tells us to expect good to come from Pip's relationship—his being "regularly bound" even, as well as "riveted"—to Magwitch.

Pip narrator finds pleasure—sometimes even comic pleasure—in associating himself with Magwitch in these early scenes. These associations become for us, upon reflection, proofs of what Pip has learned in his life: not just that in this perverse world there is nothing necessarily wrong or bad in being like a criminal, but more that it is in fact good to love someone like Magwitch.

Dickens loads adventure with value, and with meaning. When Joe takes Pip upon his shoulders to follow the soldiers chasing Magwitch, Pip "treasonably" whispers to Joe, "I hope . . . we shan't find them," and Joe whispers back, "I'd give a shilling if they had cut and run, Pip" (65). The law—"the outraged majesty of the law," as it is called here and in other Dickens novels—is not so important as to overrule or outweigh human compassion. There are values and meanings in life that transcend the limited, defensive understandings of the law. And the argument of this novel is in every way against defensiveness as a way of life.

When Magwitch is captured—he hasn't defended himself, finally, or tried to run away—the adventure is at an end, but the scene extends. Magwitch doesn't look at Pip, but he turns suddenly to the sergeant and speaks: "I wish to say something respecting this escape. It may prevent some persons laying under suspicion alonger me." What Magwitch has to say is a confession. Instead of excusing or defending himself, he claims Pip's theft as his own. "A man can't starve," he says; "at least *I* can't. I took some wittles, up at the willage over yonder."Discovering Joe as Pip's blacksmith, Magwitch apologizes for his supposed theft: "I'm sorry to say, I've eat your pie" (70). Joe's reply, however, forgives the theft: "We don't know what you have done, but we wouldn't have you starved to death for it, poor miserable fellow-creatur.—Would us, Pip?" (71).

Magwitch assumes Pip's guilt for thieving, and then Joe forgives him for it: more than forgives him, gives him what was stolen, as a Christmas gift. Quickly and easily and naturally, Joe's kindness forges a Christmas gift for Magwitch; and Magwitch, the supposedly "hardened" criminal, responds again with emotion: "The something that I had noticed before clicked in the man's throat again, and he turned his back" (71).

Several years ago one of my students asked me what this "click" was in Magwitch's throat, and why the first time Pip narrator mentions it he says that Magwitch "clicked . . . as if he had works in him like a clock, and was going to strike" (50).[37] I knew what the sound was—could imitate it even—but I had never stopped to consider what caused Magwitch to make it, or why Pip heard it as like the noise a clock makes when it is about to strike. My student proposed that the noise of that catch in the throat was caused by what Magwitch felt—and that Pip the child thought of clockworks because he didn't expect such a response from Magwitch. Pip had no way of knowing, as a child, how important his simple loyalty could be to such a man.

When "the something that I had noticed before"—clockworks, again—"clicked in [Magwitch's] throat" in response to Joe's kindness, and that "hardened" man "turned his back" to hide his tears, this first episode of the novel is made whole, as meaning rather than adventure. The repetition of this gesture marks these opening chapters as a unit of understanding. The understanding is first Magwitch's, and then Pip narrator's. For Magwitch, this small but significant whole marks the end of the first part of his life, and gives direction and meaning to the second part. For Pip narrator, the repetition of Magwitch's gesture frames this first episode as something to be understood: something which he understands, but which his child self has yet to learn, or find the meaning in.

I suggested earlier that Pip, though a "sensitive" child (92), is careful not to pay any attention to the feelings of others. "My sister's bringing up," Pip narrator says, "had made me sensitive"; what she has made him sensitive to is personal "injustice." As a child, he says, he "nursed" this sensitivity, "communing . . . with it, in a solitary and unprotected way," and indulging in self-pity in the process of that alienated and lonely communion. That Pip has become acutely aware of his own feelings is demonstrated in the opening paragraphs of the novel, in his "first most broad and vivid impression of the identity of things"— which "impression" has as its center and source Pip's sense of himself as alien. By becoming so "sensitive" to himself and to the injustices committed against him—by his sister and by life itself—Pip becomes thoroughly alienated and learns, for all his sensitivity, not to notice other people's feelings.

Like Magwitch, then, Pip is "hardened." And "hardened" people will make mistakes. What I propose to pursue now is the twin course of Pip's and Magwitch's mistakes, toward their conclusion.

When Pip and Magwitch part at the end of chapter 5, Magwitch goes back to the prison-ship, which Pip narrator calls "a wicked Noah's ark" (71). At the end of the next chapter Pip himself is taken off, "delivered over to Mr. Pumblechook . . . as if he were the Sheriff," to be taken to Miss Havisham's. A wicked Noah's ark doesn't protect or save those it takes in; it is a prison-ship, not a refuge. Likewise,

Miss Havisham's house is not a refuge, but a prison, and it saves no one.

Magwitch has been "in jail and out of jail, in jail and out of jail" (360), and knows what prisons are. Pip, however, has neither that experience nor that knowledge; and though Miss Havisham's windows are barred and shuttered, he doesn't recognize Satis House as a prison, or life there as but another form of dehumanizing punishment. He doesn't recognize the lack of feeling there, in Miss Havisham and Estella, or see himself, under the influence of that place, becoming unfeeling toward Joe and Biddy. When Magwitch returns to the Hulks, he knows what that means: prison, degradation, dehumanization. But rather than being further hardened by his return there, Magwitch returns a different man, "softened" by his brief experience out on the marshes, with Pip.

When, at the end of their first meeting on the marshes, Pip said "Goo-good night, sir" to Magwitch, the response he received was anything but friendly: "Much of that!" was the reply, as Magwitch looked out over "the cold wet flat" where he was to spend that night. And thinking perhaps of what being human means, under such circumstances, he muttered to himself, "I wish I was a frog. Or a eel" (38)—something which could be at home in that place. When Pip has "stood [his] friend," however, bringing him food and "pitying" him for his circumstances, Magwitch changes. He discovers human ambition—or, rather, the ambition to be human. And though he is imprisoned again, that next night, and then transported, Magwitch's life is different now. Henceforth Magwitch will live his life for Pip.

Magwitch's resolution to make Pip a gentleman, though good in its generous intention, is wrongheadedly ignorant. It is further corrupted by Magwitch's desire to avenge himself in the genteel world by using his boy. Though Magwitch has "lived rough, that [Pip] should live smooth," and "worked hard, that [Pip] should be above work" (337), his "making a gentleman on" Pip is a terrible mistake. The irony of the situation is that, once again, Pip and Magwitch are twins: this time in their misunderstanding of what a "gentleman" is.

Magwitch derives his definition of a "gentleman," unfortunately, from his experience with Compeyson, the only gentleman he has ever known. He can distinguish the particularly bad traits in Compeyson's character—that he is a swindler with "no more heart than a iron file," an unfeeling man "as cold as death" with "the head of the Devil" (362)—and he knows that he doesn't want his gentleman to develop such a character. What remains after he has separated these traits from his idea of a gentleman, however, is but a short list of questionable recommendations and accomplishments. Compeyson has attended "a public boarding-school and [has] learning" (361); and because he has "been to the school" he has "schoolfellows as was in this position, and in that," and he belongs to "clubs and societies" (365). Compeyson has "the ways of gentlefolks" and is "a smooth one to talk," good at "speech-making" (361, 365). He has money, or knows how to get it; and he knows how to use money to get what else he wants.

For Magwitch, then, what being a "gentleman" means is all a matter of possessions and "the ways of gentlefolks," and thus he is satisfied with his Pip when he sees him in London. A gentleman must have "no mud on *his* boots." He must "have horses" instead: "Horses to ride, horses to drive, and horses for his servants to ride and drive as well" (346–47). Magwitch admires Pip's watch—"a gold 'un, and a beauty: that's a gentleman's, I hope"—and his ring—"A diamond all set round with rubies; *that's* a gentleman's, I hope" (338). Examining Pip's "fine and beautiful linen" and his clothes, he congratulates him: "better ain't to be got," he says (338). He is impressed by Pip's lodgings as "fit for a lord" (337–38) and by his library, too: "your books . . . mounting up, on their shelves, by the hundreds!" (338). As Magwitch understands the idea, a gentleman must live by money, and let his money determine his class: "You shall show money with lords for wagers, and beat 'em" (338).

Finally Magwitch wonders if Pip might not be in love: "Isn't there bright eyes somewheres, wot you love the thoughts on?" he asks. If there are, then—clearly—a gentleman like Pip should expect to purchase them: "They shall be yourn, dear boy, if money can buy 'em. Not that a gentleman like you, so well set up as you, can't win 'em off his own game; but money shall back you!" (338).

Magwitch's notion of a gentleman has been money-defined since even before he began to dream of "mak[ing] a gentleman" (337) and being "the owner of sich" (339). When he meets Pip in London, Magwitch finds that his dream has come true. More, he discovers that Pip shares both his idea of what a gentleman is and his idea of how a gentleman can be made.

We cringe, surely, when Magwitch describes his dream to Pip. It began well, with the wonderful selflessness of his "gratitude" to Pip—that's what Pip calls it, in his condescending pride, before he recognizes what that gratitude has done for and to him. "You acted noble, my boy," Magwitch says, referring to that day when Pip "stood [his] friend" (360). But Magwitch's generous appreciation of Pip's nobility was corrupted, early on, by his ignorance of what a real gentleman could be—what true gentility would be—and by a desire for a kind of revenge on the world that has made him a "warmint."

When he found himself scorned in his society by those above him, it was "a recompense" to Magwitch "to know in secret that I was making a gentleman" (339). Colonists "might fling dust over me as I was walking," he says, or call him an "ignorant common fellow" and a "convict," but his dream for Pip—of "making a better gentleman" than they are, and being that gentleman's "owner"—solaces him: "This way I kep myself going" (339). He tells Pip that his "pleasure" now will be in seeing his gentleman "spend his money like a gentleman": That'll be *my* pleasure," he says; "*My* pleasure 'ull be fur to see him do it." But his pleasure in Pip isn't everything that Pip means to him. Magwitch is also using his gentleman. And he concludes with a curse for everyone from "the judge in his wig, to the colonist a stirring up the dust." "Blast you all!" he cries; "blast you every one . . . I'll show you a better gentleman than the whole kit on you put together" (347).

The Pip whom Magwitch finds matches Magwitch's distorted expectations. Without even having any instructions from Magwitch, Pip has managed to become exactly the kind of gentleman his "owner" wanted. He is wearing a "gentleman's" gold watch and a "gentleman's" ring, is dressed in "fine and beautiful clothes and has lodgings "fit for a lord" (337–38). If he has yet to avenge Magwitch for the insults of rude colonists, it is only because he hasn't met those wretches yet: his delight in his silly triumph over Trabb's boy—"my first decided experience of the stupendous power of money was, that it had morally laid upon his back, Trabb's boy" (178)—and his name for his servant at Barnard's Inn, "the Avenger" (241 ff.), are proof of his bad intentions. And when Magwitch proposes that Pip can buy love if he wants to, we know, as Pip does, that such is precisely what he has himself supposed he was doing with his expectations all along.

I suggested earlier that Pip is set up for his mistaken respect for money by Mrs. Joe's and Pumblechook's example. He doesn't like them, but he recognizes that they have power, and that compared to them Joe, for all his goodness, is powerless. Mrs. Joe and Pumblechook both respect money, and their respect for it teaches such to Pip and leads him to expect it to give him power. When Pip visits Miss Havisham's for the first time, he falls in love with money and with Estella. This complex infatuation makes him discontented, both with himself and with his home. Pip's misery at being "ashamed of home" (134, 136) persists for some time. "Dissatisfied, and uncomfortable," he is not "happy" with himself and grows more and more "disgusted with [his] calling and with [his] life" (155). When Jaggers finally arrives and announces Pip's "great expectations" (165), Pip is ready to leave his village, the forge, Joe and his friendship all at once. Fortune awaits him, in London; and the fortune that will eventually purchase Estella must mean happiness. When Jaggers tells him, "the sooner you leave here—as you are to be a gentleman—the better" (169), Pip agrees.

As Pip goes to bed that night he is surprised: he feels it "very sorrowful and strange," he says, "that this first night of my bright fortunes should be the loneliest I had ever known" (172). The second night is "as lonely and unsatisfying as the first" (176). When, at the end of a week, he leaves for London, he is still not happy with his prospects and breaks into tears as he leaves the village (186).

The source of Pip's discomfort, now, is not home, but leaving home. It is not the frustration of loving Estella hopelessly—he has hope now, however mistaken it may be—that causes his dissatisfaction. The source of this surprising sorrow is his leaving Joe. The first time Pip "parted from" Joe, it was to go to Miss Havisham's. He went there, however, under duress, wondering "why on earth I was going to play at Miss Havisham's, and what on earth I was expected to play at" (83). He leaves Joe now, willfully and intentionally. He knows why he is going to London, and what he is expected to play at there; but that doesn't ease his dissatisfaction at all.

It is not guilt that Pip feels. There is as yet nothing very important for Pip to feel guilty about, at least not in his relationship with Joe. What Pip feels as his discomfort is the agony of "parting," of being "parted." Pip's dreams the night before he leaves are of "fantastic failures of journeys," taken in "coaches . . . having in the traces, now dogs, now cats, now pigs, now men—never horses" (185). He can't imagine going to London, and thus all night those crazy coaches go "to wrong places instead of to London" (185).

In his small vanity Pip has "told Joe that [he] wished to walk away all alone" (185). He does so, "looking back [to see] Joe throwing an old shoe after [him] and Biddy throwing another old shoe." Biddy "put[s] her apron to her face" then, and Joe shouts a husky "Hooroar!" (186). And Pip is gone, free. As he walks away, he thinks, "it was easier to go than I had supposed it to be . . . it would never have done to have had an old shoe thrown after the coach, in the sight of all the High-street." He whistles as he walks, and at first "made nothing of going" (186).

But as the morning comes on, Pip senses that "the mists were solemnly rising, as if to show [him] the world." In part because he is unready for the world—unready to be what is called "free" in it—and in part because of his balked, unfriendly parting from Joe, Pip suddenly breaks "into tears" and says a much more feeling good-bye to his "dear, dear friend" than he had said at the forge. Pip narrator then comments: "I was better after I had cried, than before—more sorry, more aware of my ingratitude, more gentle. If I had cried before, I should have had Joe with me then" (186). This observation doesn't mean that Pip would have taken Joe to London with him, or that he would not have gone to London. He knows that "the world [lies] spread before [him]" now, and perhaps he even knows that he must go on into it: that returning to the forge, to stay, would not at all alleviate his discomfort. When he thinks, aboard the coach, that he might "get down . . . and walk back," he isn't thinking of forgoing London, but of having "another evening at home, and a better parting" (186).

Eventually it becomes "too late and too far to go back," so Pip goes on: "the mists had all solemnly risen now, and the world lay spread before me" (186). But the world, even at its distracting best, doesn't on its own or by itself resolve problems for us, or help us to lose them. "Partings"—like Pip's here at the end of the "first stage" of his "expectations"—are perhaps the most difficult problems for us humans; and awkwardly, as Joe will later remind Pip, they are what "life is made of" (246). Pip's unhappiness at parting from Joe as he leaves for London is not resolved by his arriving there. The resolution to that discomfort is a long and painful way away, for Pip. The road to happiness—to what for Dickens is the greatest expectation—is much longer than the five-hour journey from the village on the edge of the marshes to the great city in the midst of the widespread world.

Magwitch's happiness started with Pip's act of kindness—their conversation out on the marshes—that Magwitch saw as friendship. Raised a "warmint" (340), he had never known friendship until Pip "stood [his] friend." Pip's unhappiness started in earnest shortly after that encounter, when he met Magwitch's daughter at Satis House. Magwitch may have found "pleasure" in dreaming of making Pip a gentleman, and he may find pleasure—does find it, surely—in seeing his gentleman "son" become such in London. But Magwitch's happiness—something much larger than mere pleasure—is complete only when Pip at last can stand by him again, much more seriously his friend, and can accept Magwitch's friendship, as a gentleman should.

When Pip sees Magwitch, dying, as "a man who had meant to be my benefactor, and who had felt affectionately, gratefully, and generously, towards me with great constancy," he sees in him "a much better man than I had been to Joe" (456–47). Recognizing this, he both accepts Magwitch's friendship and begins his own. "When I took my place by Magwitch's side," he says, "I felt that that was my place henceforth while he lived" (456). From this new perspective, the widespread world begins to make more sense for Pip, and he, too, starts toward happiness.

Great Expectations is a remarkably subversive book, particularly in our time. In Dickens's own time *Bleak House* was objected to as subversive, and Dickens was admonished by reviewers for having written it. It attacked the idea of law, the "system" that supposedly made civilization work. It reproached lawyers as parasites, and philanthropists as little better. But we have become accustomed to a system of law that makes no attempt at justice, and we expect—teach!—parasitism as a part of the capitalist ethic. *Bleak House* is a comic novel, at best, for us; more likely it is just silly—or dumb. G. B. Shaw wrote, in the 1930s, that Dickens's *Little Dorrit* was "a more seditious book than *Das Kapital.*"[38] We have survived *Little Dorrit*, however; like *Bleak House*, it is probably more comedy or silliness than social criticism for our time. Dickens's representative governmental institution in *Little Dorrit* is the Circumlocution Office, which produces "red tape" and operates on the principle of "How Not To Do It." But we have become used to circumlocution. From the perspective of modern wisdom, that Dickens wasted his energy writing against the Barnacles who mismanage government was pretty dumb. Of course that's the way the system operates—and only a fool or an idealistic kid would bother to object. We accept governmental and bureaucratic incompetence; we expect corruption and self-serving. "How Not To Do It" becomes a company—"Howe Knott, Incorporated"—and is listed on the stock exchange. Anyone who doesn't know that hasn't been to school: literally. The educational establishment employs more Tite-Barnacles than the Circumlocution Office could ever have handled. The Vice-President becomes the Provost, so he can hire Vice-Provosts. Superintendents grow crops of Assistant Superintendents, Deans grow Associate Deans, Chairmen grow Associate Chairman—and education gets lost. "How Not To Do It" becomes the subject matter, and diplomas of all sorts credential those who learn it well. Instead of protesting, we pop our national corks to celebrate. *Little Dorrit* isn't at all subversive, for us.

But *Great Expectations* may still be subversive. Subtly, but clearly and earnestly—thanks to Pip narrator—the novel attacks money and what money buys. In so doing, it attacks our modern class society. To attack Sir Leicester Dedlock, in *Bleak House*, for his fear of the new monied class was radical in 1852; but we believe in money today so wholeheartedly that we find Sir Leicester not just a "magnificent refrigerator" but a silly old fossil. To object to governmental incompetence—intentional incompetence, even—was presumably a critical perspective in 1856; but today that's what we expect, and accept. As we have grown to accept corruption we have grown more attached to the principle corrupter, money, and more attached to the things that money can buy. We try to call these things "the good," and we try to justify our greed for them as but greed for the good life. But we are still a bit uneasy, thankfully, in our argument. Wealth and success don't seem to guarantee happiness, even in a world custom-made and behavior-modified—programmed—for such a result. Wealth and success may not be the good, after all.

Great Expectations attacks our idea of what is good, and what makes the good life: and money is at the center of that attack. You probably shouldn't be reading this little book, and you certainly should not have read *Great Expectations*. The values Dickens argues in this novel aren't our values. Money, in our society, is supposed to make you happy. Portable property—Wemmick's notion of the sine qua non—is supposed to be the representation of God in this mortal world.

But money is worthless in a *mortal* world: and that is Dickens's point. Happiness is the only thing that makes mortal life worthwhile. And happiness is a social pleasure, not a selfish one. That Pip has never experienced such unhappy nights as the first two of his "great expectations" tells us—and should have told him—that those expectations were wrong: not because they were going to take him out into the wide world, but because of what he expected to do in that wide world with his mortal life.

The reason *Great Expectations* remains a serious—and subversive—novel for us is that we can still feel the frustration that comes from the mistakes we make in our personal lives, even though we have given up on order and decency in the great mess we call society. Because of this—because we make mistakes, and sometimes even recognize them as such—Pip's mistakes register critically for us. Perhaps the reason Pip character is so uncomfortable and disturbing for us— more uncomfortable than unlikable, more disturbing than disgusting—is that he is so much like us: too much like us. Pip narrator may dislike his character self at times, perhaps even feel disgust for his miserable younger self wallowing "impatiently" in his misery and "disgusted . . . with [his] life" (155). But we have Pip narrator to soften Pip character for us—by having survived him so well. Dickens works through our relationship with Pip narrator, in having him speak directly to us about the resemblances between our lives and his on one occasion—"Pause you who read this, and think for a moment of the long chain . . . that would never have bound you" (101)—and later by having him generalize from his experience to what should be our own: "Heaven knows we need never be ashamed of our tears, for they are rain upon the blinding dust of earth, overlying our hard hearts" (186). We accept Pip's wisdom in part because it is kind, and in part because it knows from experience so much like our own.

In novels like *Bleak House* and *Little Dorrit* Dickens criticized institutions in society, and generalized them symbolically as "the system." In *Great Expectations* what he attacks is not the idea of social institutions, but rather that of social values. We have long since accepted worthless and corrupt institutions, and have learned to pretend to have a society in spite of them. We can acknowledge that "the system" itself is perverse, or worse, but still claim progress and civilized achievement. Because this is the way we live now, critical or satiric responses to our institutions are no longer disturbing: we thrive anyway, it seems, so we make jokes about them—like the jokes we make about banana peels. But we don't joke about our values—yet. And *Great Expectations*'s attack upon our values—on the corruption of our values—must still register as seditious for those of us who would accept the world we live in as the arbiter of the good.

Wemmick is at the worst comic, if we intend to become Wemmicks; his belief in the value of "portable property" over the value of friendship, however, is a serious matter for both Pip narrator and Dickens. For those who care about human values, whatever is good about Wemmick is finally corrupted by his preference for money. When Wemmick laments, at Magwitch's death, "the sacrifice of so much portable property," Pip responds, "What *I* think of, Wemmick, is the poor owner of the property." But Wemmick does not agree: "Of course there can be no objection to your being sorry for him. . . . But what I look at, is this. . . . I do not think he could have been saved. That's the difference between the property and the owner, don't you see?" (461). If in reading the novel we feel uneasy or disappointed at what happens to Magwitch's portable property, we belong with Wemmick, in terms of values, not with Pip.

Jaggers is a grotesque creature, not to be taken seriously, if we plan to live our lives as corruptly as he does. Is it squeamishness that makes him wash his hands with scented soap every time he finishes a piece of business with a client? Do we—or our friends whom we admire—need to wash our hands like that? Maybe what we do isn't quite so bad. Or maybe nothing can corrupt us—no matter what we do. Or maybe we accept our corruption.

And Pip? His guilt? Pip isn't a criminal: why should he feel guilty? Magwitch is the criminal, not Pip. But Magwitch insists that he has paid for his crime, and though he is breaking the law by returning to England he feels no guilt at all for that. What's more, Pip narrator agrees with him—and Pip character eventually accepts the legitimacy of Magwitch's attitude. Pip character even stands this criminal's friend when he is captured, imprisoned, tried, and convicted.

What Pip character learns through the course of his experience with

Magwitch makes him finally more like his convict—in a serious sense—rather than less so. As we approach the end of the novel we discover a new reason for Pip narrator's teasing us with all those comic parallels and associations between his child self and Magwitch. By the end of the novel Pip—who began the novel never having known his father—knows father as well as friend in Magwitch. And as Magwitch dies, a "gentleman" in spite of his situation or social station, "softened" and made gentle by affection, his gentleman son Pip tells him that his daughter is "a lady"—and that he loves her (470).

Pip's story begins with Magwitch, out on the marshes. When Magwitch reappears in Pip's life, in London, Pip asks him to tell his own story, which he does. That story becomes doubly entwined with Pip's own, and Pip soon discovers that he knows more of Magwitch's story than Magwitch does himself. When he takes this knowledge to Jaggers, for verification, he gets, of course, but little satisfaction. He does, however, get some advice.

Pip's knowledge is a knowledge of relationships: of who Magwitch is, and who Molly is, and who their daughter is. Pip doesn't know what to do with this knowledge, however, now that he has it: "What purpose I had in view," Pip narrator says, "when I was hot on tracing out and proving Estella's parentage, I cannot say. It will presently be seen that the question was not before me in a distinct shape, until it was put to me by a wiser head than my own" (420).

Jaggers's is the "wiser head" that gives the question shape for Pip, and advises him. "For whose sake," Jaggers asks, "would you reveal the secret? For the father's? . . . For the mother's? . . . For the daughter's?" (426). According to Jaggers's wisdom, the answer each time is negative: there can be no reason to reveal this information to any of the parties involved. Though Jaggers's arguments for Pip's not divulging his secret are weak—they are based in the ideas of safety and social status—his advice seems indeed to be sound, and Pip accepts it temporarily. The context Jaggers sets for the question is one of utility: "For whose sake would you reveal the secret?" And at this point Pip can see no use for his knowledge for anyone.

As Magwitch lies dying, however, Pip finds a wonderful use for what he has learned—or for part of it, at any rate. What he has learned of Magwitch's relationships enables him to give Magwitch back his daughter, as a "lady," and at the same time to complete his own relationship to him, as his friend and son. Pip gives his "Dear Magwitch" (469) happiness, and Magwitch dies, holding Pip's hand.

Nine

Hands, Chains, Parts and Partings, Clicks

When Magwitch first appeared to Pip he "seized [him] by the chin" (36). When he grabbed Pip, as he sat on that "high tombstone, trembling," he "took [him] by both arms" and tilted him over backwards, farther and farther—tilted him until finally Pip "clung to him with both hands" (37) in terror.

Dickens is most often an obsessive writer. Recurring images, themes, and ideas all develop out of his obsessions. In this novel hands are a wonderful obsession for him—for Pip narrator, anyway—and the recurrence of the word creates and carries meaning from beginning to end.[39] Typically, such obsessions grow and develop through the course of a novel. Sometimes, as you look at the manuscript, Dickens seems almost to be encouraging his obsessions; sometimes you sense that you have caught him discovering the obsession, and determining to exploit it in the chapters yet to come. In *Great Expectations* hands are the most obvious of the recurring motifs, the easiest to follow as well as to make meaning of. If we can work through some of the more significant references to hands in the novel—there are more than three hundred, altogether—then we should be able to find the patterns of several other ideas and themes that develop, through the repetition of words and image-words.

I have long used as a working rule in reading Dickens's novels that anything which is repeated must have some special meaning. The mark of any great work of art—a painting, a piece of music, a novel—is that it makes sense: that all the parts cohere, and that together they mean something to our senses. I am not arguing for a strictly intellectual response to art; such an argument would sterilize art, and reduce it to academic proportions. But works of art do have meaning, and they work by a logic. More often than not, art uses the logic of the imagination rather than the logic of reason—but art still makes logical sense. When the poet Dylan Thomas was told—wrongly, erroneously—that surrealism "has no meaning," he was outraged that people were calling him a surrealist. When we excuse so many of Salvador Dali's pretentious but meaningless tricks as surrealistic painting, we are extending the error. Art has meaning: it makes sense. One of the tests for meaning that we can use with a great work of art is the significance of its details. If there are irrelevancies, parts that don't mean anything or make any sense, then the work of art is flawed. When the artist repeats an image or a theme or a descriptive detail, you should expect the repetition to signal something. If it doesn't, there is something wrong with the work of art.

Repetitions in *Great Expectations* make sense. More than that, they mark the development or progress of meaning and understanding in the novel. In *Great Expectations* repetitions function like links of a chain, binding together as meaning the various pieces of Pip's story—and that chain is itself one of the images repeated in his story. Before we deal with chains, however, and parts and partings and clicks, let's examine the way Dickens uses hands, from the first chapter to the last, to make meaning for the novel.

When Magwitch arrives in London, midway through the novel, and comes up the stairs at Barnard's Inn to meet Pip, Pip sees with "a stupid kind of amazement, that he was holding out both his hands to me" (332). Pip questions him—"inhospitably enough"—but lets him enter; and having entered, Magwitch "once more [holds] out both his hands to me" (333). Pip cries, "What do you mean?" Magwitch responds by miming a scene from their past—of a convict, out on the marshes—and then again holds out "both his hands" (334). This time, "reluctantly," Pip gives Magwitch his hands in return. When Magwitch has told Pip what their relationship is—that he is the source of Pip's great expectations, and his "second father"—he takes Pip's hands again, and kisses them, causing Pip's blood to run cold with terror (338). Magwitch "[lays] his hand on [Pip's] shoulder," and Pip shudders (339). When Magwitch is ready to go to bed, he once more takes

Pip "by both hands to give [him] good night"—and Pip's "blood again [runs] cold" (340).

A great deal happens between the opening of *Great Expectations* and this scene, and a great deal more happens between this scene and the conclusion. Much of what Pip narrator represents as his character self's growth—and thus as his understanding both of his own story and of life itself—is definable in and through the continuous reference to hands.

The next time we see Magwitch "clasping [Pip's] hands" (392) is as Pip leaves him at Mrs. Whipple's. "I don't like to leave you here," says Pip; and his narrator self comments, "I thought of the first night of his return . . . when I little supposed my heart could ever be as heavy and anxious at parting from him as it was now" (392).

When Magwitch has been captured and lies "shackled" again, as he was when Pip first met him, Pip lets Magwitch hold his hand and promises, "I will never stir from your side. . . . Please God, I will be as true to you, as you have been to me" (457). During the short weeks between Magwitch's capture and his death, he and Pip communicate with their hands; Magwitch's injuries make it difficult for him to speak, so he substitutes "slight pressures on [Pip's] hand" for words, which Pip can "understand . . . very well" (469).

When Magwitch has "spoken his last words," he indicates by "touch" that "he wishes to lift [Pip's] hand, and lay it on his breast." "I understood," Pip says, "and laid it there, and he . . . put both his hands upon it" (469). As Pip tells him about Estella, Magwitch's responses are "a gentle pressure on my hand" (469), then "a stronger pressure on my hand," and finally his kissing Pip's hand:

> With a last faint effort, which would have been powerless but for my yielding to it and assisting it, he raised my hand to his lips. Then, he gently let it sink upon his breast again, with his own hands lying on it. (470)

Pip's last communication with Magwitch is his giving him his hand, literally: "yielding" and "assisting" him to hold it.

Pip's learning the language of hands runs parallel to the rest of his learning in *Great Expectations*. Pip narrator's obsessive focus on hands carries, symbolically, his understanding of relationships. It begins with his remembering his five little brothers—who "gave up" early in this life, and deserted him—as having "been born on their backs with their hands in their trousers-pockets" (36). His first clinging to Magwitch "with both hands" (37) is not in itself evidence of a relationship, or of an understanding of what relationships are, though it does introduce the motif in the novel. When put together with later images of Pip's and Magwitch's hands, however, Pip's clinging to him with his hands in chapter 1 perhaps shows us Pip narrator's special foreshadowing of their future friendship. The first use of "hands" to describe a relationship occurs at the beginning of the second chapter, as Pip tells us of his having been "brought up by hand." This relationship, so described, is not a comfortable one—it is almost a negative one—but it tell us something important about Pip's early perception of the world he lives in.

Life is essentially a matter of relations, and relationships. The body as substance is but a body, neither alive nor significantly dead. Just as in *David Copperfield* the names people give David don't mean anything to him—they tell us something of how others perceive him, but they don't tell us anything about his essential self—so in general nouns substantive are insignificant in themselves. As early as in *Nicholas Nickleby*, Dickens had found a way of dramatizing this idea, in the teachings of schoolmaster Squeers: "B-o-t-, bot, t-i-n, tin, bottin, n-e-y, ney, bottinney, noun substantive, a knowledge of plants. When [a boy] has learned that bottinney means a knowledge of plants, he goes and knows 'em" (*NN*, 155). A later character, Mark Tapley, insists that he is a "werb" (*MC*, 810), and a most active one at that. What verbs do, of course, is create relationships: and that creation is what Dickens would call proper life.

Though Mrs. Joe is Pip's "sister," she rejects that relationship to him as much as possible—which is probably why Dickens made her a whole generation older than Pip. She has brought Pip up, but she assures him that she would "never do it again!" (41). Mrs. Joe has no sense of relationship. When Pip narrator describes his being thrown at Joe, as a child, he remarks that he "often served as a connubial missile" (41), which is an appropriate representation, it seems, of Mrs. Joe's notion of marriage as a relationship. To be "brought up by hand" by Mrs. Joe is as bad as being taught by Wackford Squeers.

Mrs. Joe has "established a great reputation with herself and the neighbours" because she has "brought [Pip] up 'by hand.' " Not knowing what the expression means, but "knowing her to have a hard and heavy hand, and to be much in the habit of laying it upon her husband as well as upon [himself]," Pip supposes that he and Joe "were both brought up by hand," and that "she must have made Joe Gargery marry her by hand" (39). In the inimical atmosphere of Mrs. Joe's domain, the hand is an instrument of punishment; more generally, in these early chapters, hands are associated with wrongdoing or the results of wrongdoing. After his theft from the pantry Pip is full of remorse at "what [his] hands had done" (51). When the soldiers come to the door, the sergeant holds out "a pair of handcuffs" at Pip and places his other hand on Pip's shoulder (61). Fearing that the "handcuffs" are for him, Pip watches the soldiers' "hands" (62). The handcuffs are for Magwitch, however, not for Pip; and Magwitch absolves Pip's hands of their crime by claiming it as his own. In this act, Magwitch with his "manacled hands" frees Pip toward friendship. He and Pip are guilty together, but Magwitch frees Pip from "laying under suspicion alonger [him]" (70). The next time Magwitch uses that strange word "alonger"—the only other time in the novel—he and Pip are holding hands in the prison infirmary: "And what's best of all, " he says to Pip, "you've been more comfortable alonger me. . . . That's best of all" (469). "Alonger" is a special word, signifying relation; and it matches with both freedom and friendship as well as hands.

Holding hands is not itself friendship, however, or relation; and hands held must finally be let go. It is not the touching of hands, or their joining together, that has meaning; rather, the meaning comes from Pip narrator's understanding of the hands which touch, or join, or part. Hands, in *Great Expectations*, are not symbols; they are signs along the way of Pip's path, like "the finger-post at the end of the village" (186), by which he shows us the progress of his understanding of life.

When Pip narrator introduces Biddy to us, he introduces her as "an orphan like [him]self" who, like him, "had been brought up by hand." What he recalls his child-self noticing about her is that she was untidy, and that "her hands always wanted washing" (74). After Pip hears of his good fortune, his great expectations, he discusses with Biddy his ambitions for Joe, in terms of "his learning and his manners." Biddy is angry at Pip's insensitivity, as is Pip narrator remembering the scene. What the narrator details of Biddy's response to Pip is a very subtle commentary on the snobbery of his younger self's plans:

> "Oh, his manners! won't his manners do, then?" asked Biddy, plucking a black-currant leaf.
> "My dear Biddy, they do very well here—"
> "Oh! They *do* very well here?" interrupted Biddy, looking closely at the leaf in her hand.
> "Hear me out—but if I were to remove Joe into a higher sphere . . . they would hardly do him justice."
> "And don't you think he knows that?" asked Biddy.
> . . . .
> Biddy, having rubbed the leaf to pieces between her hands . . . the smell of a black-currant bush has ever since recalled to me that evening in the little garden by the side of the land. . . . (175)

Her plucking that black-currant leaf, looking at it "in her hand," and rubbing it to pieces "between her hands" is the gesture that carries, for Pip narrator, the sense of her understanding and his younger self's misunderstanding. Her soiling her hands with that leaf should remind us of her being his teacher, earlier, even though she, like Joe, had dirty hands.

Biddy's "hands" have been "always clean" (152) for some time now, however—ever since she came to the forge to live, in fact—and she has become both generally tidy and "pleasant" in Pip's eyes. Still, she is "common," and "not . . . like Estella" (152).

Commonness is the great curse for the young Pip, and the first indication of commonness is, as Estella teaches him, "coarse hands" (90). But coarseness, like commonness itself, is both subjective and relative. Toward the end of the novel, when Biddy kisses Pip's hand (487) on her wedding day, she doesn't seem coarse or common; and eleven years later, when Pip returns from Cairo to visit the forge once more, her gesture of kissing her baby's hand and then putting her own hand—"the good matronly hand"—into Pip's hand has, for Pip, "a very pretty eloquence to it" (490). The hands are the same; their meaning is different.

There are false hands, of course—or rather hands that mean falseness. Pumblechook's false hands want to shake Pip's—"May I—*may* I—?" (179–80)—so long as Pip has "expectations"; when Pip has been "brought low," however, Pumblechook "extend[s] his hand with a magnificently forgiving air." Pip narrator comments on "the wonderful difference between the servile manner in which he had offered his hand in my new prosperity, saying 'May I?' and the ostentatious clemency with which he . . . now exhibited the same fat five fingers" (483).

Jaggers uses his forefinger as a weapon, and his hands, soiled by his work, need constantly to be washed in scented soap. The gesture tells us that he knows the immorality of his work: like Lady Macbeth, he cannot hide his culpability from himself. Like Lady Macbeth, he is troubled by the "smell" of his guilt; and "all the perfumes of Arabia will not sweeten [his] little hand."[40] When Jaggers actually shakes hands, he does so not to prove friendship, but because it is required of him, as a formality. When Pip shakes hands with him upon the occasion of his twenty-first birthday—a formal occasion, requiring a handshake—Pip narrator comments that Jaggers "was always a remarkably short shaker" (305).

Our first clue to the problem with Wemmick's character comes at the end of his and Pip's first conversation together. Pip says, "I put out my hand, and Mr. Wemmick at first looked at it as if he thought I wanted something." Then Wemmick corrects himself, and says candidly: "To be sure. Yes. You're in the habit of shaking hands?" (197).

Wemmick only shakes hands "at last," he says—just before executions, in appreciation for the small bequests that he cherishes so under the heading of "portable property" (281–82). Though Wemmick's exception to his rule on this first meeting with—or rather, parting from—Pip has no seriously ominous meaning, Pip narrator reports the comical coincidence that immediately after he and Wemmick have "shaken hands and he was gone," he "opened a staircase window and . . . nearly beheaded [him]self, for, the lines had rotted away, and it came down like the guillotine" (197). One has to be careful, shaking hands with Wemmick: it is safe—in what it means—only at Walworth. His business handshake may get you hanged, or beheaded.

Shaking hands with an honest man is a different matter, however. When Pip meets Herbert the first time, at Miss Havisham's, they don't shake hands; they fight instead. When they meet again, in London, they don't—can't—shake hands at first, though that would be the proper thing to do, because Herbert has his arms loaded with parcels. He assures Pip, however, that though they "shall be alone together," they "shan't fight" (199). When they have managed to get the parcels settled, they recognize each other—as "the prowling boy" and "the pale young gentleman," respectively, from their fighting days—and begin immediately to become friends. Herbert "reach[es] out his hand good-humouredly," and as Pip narrator recalls it, they "shook hands warmly" (199). The good humor and warmth are important elements in this description. That this handshake, delayed first by Herbert's armload of packages and then by the testing shock of their mutual recognition, is so good-humored and warm assures us that it is honest, not mechanical or simply formal.

When Herbert comes home from his trip to Marseilles, he comes "bursting in," and as he shakes hands with Pip cries, "Handel, my dear fellow, how are you, and again how are you, and again how are you?" (354). Herbert is interrupted in this comically extravagant greeting by seeing Magwitch. Magwitch can't afford to be very trusting, so he makes Herbert put his hand upon the Bible—"Take it in your right hand," he says—before he can indulge in "shaking hands with him." But since Herbert is Pip's friend, and since he has sworn an oath not to "split in any way sumever," Magwitch accepts Herbert, shakes his hand, and promises that Pip will "make a gentleman on [him]" (354).

When Pip returns to Barnard's Inn that night, after settling Magwitch in his lodgings, Herbert receives him "with open arms," and Pip narrator comments, in response, "I had never felt before so blessedly, what it is to have a friend" (356). When Pip confides in Herbert that he is in desperate need "of taking counsel with [his] friendship and affection," he breaks down; Herbert responds by "seizing a warm grip of [Pip's] hand" (357) and offering his responsible, thoughtful, friendly assistance.

As the novel draws to its close, Herbert and Pip part again. When Herbert tells Pip that he must go to Cairo, he apologizes: "I am very much afraid I must go, Handel, when you most need me." Pip's response is wise with understanding: "Herbert, I shall always need you, because I shall always love you; but my need is no greater now than at another time" (459). Their conversation continues beyond this point, with Herbert's proposal that Pip must come join Clarriker and Co. As he suggests this, he extends "his honest hand" and tells Pip that Clara seconds him in his request, and proposes to be his "friend" as much as Herbert is. The matter isn't settled before Herbert leaves, but the two young men shake hands on the understanding of the proposal, and that's enough—for friends, for honest men.

Joe and Pip don't shake hands often, mainly because until Pip has become a gentleman their relationship is more openly affectionate than mere handshakes will sustain. Pip's more usual gesture, with Joe, is to throw his arms around Joe's neck and hug him. When Joe comes to London to visit Pip, however, he shakes Pip's hand—but in a wonderfully exaggerated fashion: "he caught both my hands and worked them straight up and down, as if I had been the last-patented Pump" (241). When Herbert enters, Pip presents Joe to him, but Herbert's having "held out his hand" to Joe gets no response (243): Joe has too much difficulty with young "gentlemen" to indulge in shaking hands with Herbert. At the end of a very short stay Joe shakes Pip's hand again (246), touches Pip "gently on the forehead," and leaves (247).

When Pip returns to the village for Mrs. Joe's funeral, he finds the undertaking establishment in charge of everything—he makes the mistake of trying to shake hands with Mr. Trabb (298) instead of handing him his hat for mourning decoration—and finds Joe seated ludicrously in state, as the chief mourner. When we compare Joe's discomfort in this scene to the discomfort that Pip caused in London, with his gentlemanly status and his gentlemanly manners, we perhaps conclude that the absurd funeral manners which Mr. Trabb enforces are no more absurd than Pip's London manners. Because of Joe's situation, communication between Pip and Joe is cramped. Pip can only "bend down and [say] to him, 'Dear Joe, how are you?' " There is nothing more. Joe tries to answer, but breaks off in mid-sentence, and having "clasped [Pip's] hand," can say no more (299).

The morning after the funeral Pip goes away again. As Pip narrator reports his departure, he shows himself to us "looking in . . . at one of the wooden windows of the forge . . . at Joe, already at work." Then, without any narrative description of his calling to Joe or going inside the forge to greet him, without any mention of what Joe does when he sees him, Pip gives us his own words: "Good-bye, dear Joe!—No, don't wipe it off—for God's sake, give me your blackened hand!" (304). There is something of repentance here, in Pip's words, and the gesture that they imply marks its significance.

Pip's hands are blackened, too—but not as a result of his working at the forge. His hands are badly burned when he tries to save Miss Havisham (416). Weeks later, after the attempt to get Magwitch away, and after Magwitch's trial and his death, Pip finally falls "very ill" (470). When he awakens from his troubled, feverish sleep, Joe is there, "[laying] his head down on the pillow" beside Pip and "put[ting] his arm round [Pip's] neck" (472). Pip narrator remembers "holding [Joe's] hand," and having "kissed his hand," and he knows that they "both felt happy" (473). But then Joe leaves him. Having "patted the coverlet" on Pip's bed "with his great good hand" (480) one Sunday night, Joe departs—without shaking hands. The note he leaves to explain his conduct—"not wishful to intrude I have departured fur you are well again dear Pip"—concludes with a postscript: "Ever the best of friends" (481).

Two more incidents involving hands and we are finished. When Pip returns to the village to tell Miss Havisham that he knows now who his benefactor is, he finds Estella there and hears her tell him that she will soon marry Bentley Drummle. Having told Pip this, Estella bids Pip good-bye: "Here is my hand," she says; "Do we part on this, you visionary boy—or man?" (377). When Pip returns to the village a dozen years later, he again visits Satis House—or rather the place where Satis House once stood—and he meets Estella there, for the last time. They speak of the past, and Estella sets this present moment in relation to what must be the future: "I little thought," she says, "that I should take leave of you in taking leave of this spot. I am very glad to do so." And then she asks, "tell me we are friends." Pip does as she requests: "We are friends," he says. She responds, "And will continue friends apart" (460). Pip takes her hand, then, and the novel is finished.

If we have read well the lesson of "hands"—the meaning that Pip narrator develops by his use of hands throughout the novel—we will make sense of these final paragraphs. Pip and Estella part, as friends: just as Pip and Magwitch parted at Magwitch's death (470); just as Pip and Herbert parted when Herbert went to Cairo (459); just as Pip and Joe parted, "ever the best of friends" (481). "Life," Joe said, shaking Pip's hand: "Life is made of ever so many partings welded together" (246).

Ten

Chains, Etc., Part 2

Dickens's creative impulse is to put things together. That is the function of the imagination: as Coleridge says, it "dissolves, diffuses, dissipates, in order to recreate . . . to idealise and to unify."[41] *David Copperfield* is a novel that puts the world together, as David's life. The classical Greek axiom, Γνῶθι σεαυτόν—"Know thyself"— is satisfied by that kind of comprehension. At the beginning of his novel David character is able to "observe, in little pieces, as it were; but as to making a net of a number of these pieces . . . that was, as yet, beyond [him]" (*DC*, 70). By the end of the novel David narrator has comprehended his world, put it all together with himself at its center, as its knowing, understanding hero, and he calls this world his "life": *David Copperfield*.

In *Our Mutual Friend* Dickens divides the function of the imagination into two parts, symbolically. He represents the critical operation of examination—the work of the imagination which "dissolves, diffuses, dissipates"—in the person of the servant whom he calls "the Analytical Chemist," or simply "the Analytical." The character whose symbolic role matches the other end of the imagination's function, "to recreate . . . to idealise and to unify," is the wonderfully comic taxidermist named Venus. He is an "articulator of skeletons," someone who puts the pieces together.

In *Great Expectations* Pip narrator does the analysis; sometimes his character-self does a bit of analysis, too. The obvious candidate for the symbolic role of putting things together is the blacksmith, Joe, who thinks of life as his work, and generalizes work as smith-work: "one man's a blacksmith, and one's a whitesmith, and one's a goldsmith, and one's a coppersmith" (246). The forge is the center of Joe's world, where he works at shaping and welding everything he meets. Literally, of course, it is Pip narrator who puts together the things he has ana-lyzed, to make sense of his life for us.

The sense of *Great Expectations*, however, is not just one of putting together pieces, or parts, as they are understood, to make a life. Unlike earlier Dickens novels, this one is not called, after its central character, "Philip Pirrip." The focus is not on Pip's life—as it was on Oliver Twist's and Nicholas Nickleby's and Barnaby Rudge's and Martin Chuzzlewit's and even David Copperfield's. The focus here is much more directly on the meaning of Pip's life as *Great Expectations*.

In *Great Expectations* the end of the analysis—what the parts get put together as—is much more fable or moral lesson than life: the focus of the novel is insistently and directly on what Pip's life means, more so than on his identity. In some sense, two of the three novels immediately preceding *Great Expectations* are even more fabular or exemplary. *Hard Times*, with its "Writing on the Wall" (*HT*, 313), and *A Tale of Two Cities* are both limited by being more fabular than dramatic, more symbolic than real. *Great Expectations*'s success is the result of its managing to be both dramatic and real at the same time that it carries such a direct moral lesson for us. It manages this thanks to the way Dickens uses the first-person narrative.

The lesson of this novel is a more philosophical one than the lesson of Dickens's earlier novels, and Pip narrator argues it for him, not in terms of putting parts together, but rather in terms of ambiguous chains and partings. Pip narrator is not just a storyteller—no narrator ever is. In addition to telling his story, Pip narrator creates rich critical meaning out of his story, which he communicates both directly in oc-casional editorial comments to us his readers, and indirectly through deeply woven patterns of image and association in the language of his narration.

"Part" is a verb in *Great Expectations*; "partings" are gerundive and participial formations from that verb. The word appears in but one scene in its substantive form. Estella gives Pip her hand and says, "Do we part on this, you visionary boy—or man? " (377). His reply rejects her intention to "part" *from* him, by claiming that she is a substantial "part" *of* him. "You are part of my existence, part of my self. . . . you cannot choose but remain part of my character, part of the little good in me, part of the evil" (378). A dozen years later, when he returns to England to visit Biddy and Joe at the forge, Biddy asks Pip if he has "forgotten her," and he answers, "My dear Biddy, I have forgotten nothing in my life that ever had a foremost place there, and little that ever had any place there" (490). The "poor dream" that Pip had, of marrying Estella, "has all gone by" (490), but she is still actively and substantially a "part" of his life; of his existence.

Otherwise, parts are not substances in *Great Expectations*. Joe may weld pieces of metal together at the forge and repair handcuffs, but that's not what the novel is about. The parts that have value are those that transcend objectively substantial existence, and assume relational significance. Octavio Paz, the modern Mexican poet and philosopher, argues that the true meaning of life is to be found in relations, not substances. In saying this, he echoes the greatest things said in the history of human thought. All great works of art say, each in its own way, that same thing. *Great Expectations* says it as beautifully and as movingly as any.

Though Joe is a blacksmith, his interests in life aren't limited to welding metal. He is not exactly a philosopher, but he is the novel's only poet; and in his prize couplet he transforms his father's rough substance—"the failings on his part"—into relations—"he were that good in his hart" (77). Because of how he understands life, Joe is even able to make his work as a blacksmith something philosophical, again transforming substance into relation: what we call "Life," Joe says, "is made of ever so many partings welded together" (246).

Relations form paradoxically. That friendship frees us is itself a paradox: both words, remember, come from the Germanic word *frei*, "to love," and from the Sanskrit *priyá*, "dear." When John Stuart Mill wrote in *On Liberty*—a work that appeared the year before *Great Expectations*—that social freedom is both greater and larger than individual freedom, his argument had an etymological base. *Social* is a word which matches well with the idea of freedom, and the idea that you can't be free by yourself. *Social* derives from the latin *socius*, "friend" or "companion"; and *socius* comes from the Sanskrit *sak*, which in its various forms means both "friend" and "to follow." Society is made up of friends following each other: and their friendship is what makes freedom possible.

Released by his "great expectations" from the articles that have "bound" him apprentice to Joe (48, 133), Pip expects to be happy. But "the first night of [his] bright fortunes" is "the loneliest [he] had ever known" (172), and the second night is no better (176). Pip's "great expectations" complete the alienation from his home that he has always felt to some extent—and alienation has nothing to do with freedom. The "small bundle of shivers growing afraid of it all and beginning to cry" whom we met in the opening paragraphs of the novel is already alone in the world, as he sees himself. Joe's friendship is incapable of overcoming Pip's sense of unwantedness and loneliness. The best he can do is promise Pip a better future, when they are partners at the forge. Joe proposes that they will have "such Larks" (54) then, and Pip expects to grow there "to manhood and independence" (134). But once Pip meets Estella and the glittering alternative to life at the forge that she and Satis House represent, he can't ever again enjoy the idea of working with Joe at the forge. Everything fails him: he is unhappy with Joe, unhappy with himself, unhappy with his home, unhappy with his life.

Pip expects his "bright fortunes" to make him happy, but from the first they don't. They release him from the forge, but they don't free him. What happiness he finds, as a young gentleman in London, derives not from his fortune but from his friendship with Herbert—and that friendship is what begins to make him free.

Magwitch has a shackle on his leg when Pip first sees him. Pip's theft of Joe's file has as its object Magwitch's setting himself free, though he turns out not to use it for such. Magwitch's leg-iron should have had no meaning for Pip, certainly none beyond the moment when he gave his convict Joe's file to use to cut it off. But it turns up, strangely, as the weapon used to attack Mrs. Joe (148). Later, when Pip is preparing to leave for London, he wanders out onto the marshes one evening and "recall[s]" that evening so long ago when Magwitch "started up from among the graves" (36) at him. But that "wretch . . . with his felon iron" belongs to another world, Pip thinks; Pip's "comfort" is "that it happened a long time ago . . . and that he was dead to me, and might be veritably dead into the bargain" (173). Magwitch is not dead, however, nor is the past; and when Magwitch appears in London, Pip images for himself his horrible situation in terms of "chains": the leg-iron, transformed, becomes the "gold and silver chains" (340) of Pip's fortune, and he feels with shame that he is "chained to" Magwitch now (346).

Chains, like manacles and handcuffs and leg-irons, are not ordinarily pleasant things to contemplate. The gibbet with its "chains . . . which had once held a pirate" (39, 47), the Hulks themselves, "barred and moored by massive rusty chains" so that they seem "to be ironed like the prisoners" (71), are images of horror. But Pip narrator uses the same image, ambiguously, to argue how a life is made: "Pause you who read this, and think for a moment of the long chain of iron or gold, of thorns or flowers, that would never have bound you, but for the formation of the first link on one memorable day" (101). "Life," here, is made of links "welded together"—to borrow Joe's words. The question is not whether one is bound or not, but whether one's "chain" is "of iron or gold, of thorns or flowers."

Pip's happiness in life comes from those good bonds, the chains of feeling. It comes from his friendship with Herbert, from the relationship that he learns to make with Magwitch, from the bond of love that ties him to Joe and Biddy, and from the love or friendship with which he and Estella part at the end of the novel.

Life is not circumstance, but meaning. When Magwitch is sentenced to death along with thirty-one other people, Pip narrator notes that the sunlight coming through the windows of the court makes "a broad shaft of light between the two-and-thirty and the Judge, linking both together, and perhaps reminding some among the audience how both were passing on, with absolute equality, to the greater Judgment" (467). The "linking" is Pip's; it makes a larger community than the Judge can comprehend, and becomes Pip's judgment, then, upon the system of justice. The boy who supplied his convict with a file, and who hoped—"treasonably"—that he wouldn't be recaptured, has grown up to think similarly treacherous thoughts. The scene of Magwitch's sentencing is a vivid one: the room is filled with "sheriffs with great chains and nosegays, other civic geegaws and monsters, criers, ushers, a great gallery full of people" (466) as well as thirty-two condemned men and women and a Judge. The Judge "must single out" Magwitch "for special address." Pip narrator doesn't comment editorially on what the Judge says about Magwitch; he depends upon our understanding both Magwitch and his story better than the Judge can understand them. The only critical comment Pip narrator makes to convert these circumstances into meaning is that observation of the "shaft of light between the two-and-thirty and the Judge, linking both together."

Earlier, when Pip visits Jaggers's house in Gerrard Street to receive a brief communication from Miss Havisham, he forges a connection, accidentally, between two images, and discovers suddenly who Estella's mother is. He sees Molly's hands move as Estella's have moved, when she was knitting, and makes a connection. He explains his discovery as the result of a linking: "I thought of how one link of association had helped that identification in the theatre, and how such a link, wanting before, had been riveted for me now" (403). What is "riveted" together to form this "link" is not itself significant; the significance is in the relationship—literally, this time, a relationship!—created by the meaningful linkage. Such links are called metaphors. And metaphors carry the meanings that the imagination makes out of life.

Neither Pip's response to the Judge's condemnation of Magwitch nor his discovery that Molly is Estella's mother can in any direct way give Pip much pleasure. These two incidents are important, however, as examples of Pip's new and growing sympathetic understanding of the world around him. The selfish Pip thought only of himself; now his notice of the world around him lets him think of others. Pip's "first most vivid and broad impression of the identity of things" showed him the world as it related to him: he had no other relations. Now he sees other people's worlds, and finds meaningful relations in them. Pip's quiet protest against the Judge is his defense of Magwitch. His recognition of Molly as Estella's mother occurs in such a way as to underline what Pip now understands about suffering.

When Pip spoke with Estella at Satis House the previous time, she sat calmly knitting as she assured him she was going to marry Bentley Drummle. Pip knew that this was folly and cried out against it; Estella could only tell him that she had been raised to commit just such folly, that she was "not able to comprehend" what "love" is (376). As she spoke, Estella was calm, unfeeling, cold; Pip was deeply anguished. The focus of the scene, finally, was not on Estella's pathetic lack of feeling, but on Pip's pain and sorrow. A short time later, when Pip is reminded of Estella by Molly, the connection comes from Jaggers's unfeeling comments about Estella's marriage in Molly's presence: the "link" is "riveted" by the connection of "Estella's name to [Molly's] fingers with their knitting action" (403). This knowledge doesn't give Pip character pleasure—it has nothing to do with his pleasure in life, directly. What it shows us is Pip's new or newly recovered ability to feel and make connections outside himself. His discovery of meaning, here, is the first part of that sympathetic understanding that will eventually let him know how to give Magwitch back his lost daughter, as a "lady" (470), before he dies.

When Pip first met Magwitch, he had no way of responding to him sympathetically. His experience had taught him nothing about being kind to monsters rising up out of the marshes, or "warmints." When Magwitch "clicked . . . as if he had works in him" and "smeared his ragged rough sleeve over his eyes" (50) Pip didn't understand: he didn't expect such emotion from such a man. When Magwitch responded to Joe's Christmas gift to him—his giving Magwitch that pie, and calling him a "poor miserable fellow-creatur"—with another click, and then "turned his back" (71), Pip still didn't understand.

When Magwitch appears in London and tells Pip who he is, and how "proud" he is of his boy-become-gentleman, Pip is horrified and disgusted. Moved by seeing in the flesh what he has "looked slowly forward to" for so many years, Magwitch again "draw[s] his sleeve over his eyes and forehead," and "the click came in his throat which I well remembered." This time Pip character knows what the gesture and the sound indicate, but he rejects it: "he was all the more horrible to me," Pip says, "that he was so much in earnest" (338) as to show emotion.

Pip is old enough now, and experienced enough in the world, that he should be able to appreciate Magwitch's emotion, even if he cannot like the man. But except for Herbert, Pip doesn't have any selfless relationships, and thus for all of his twenty-three years has no larger appreciation of the world than he had when he was seven and first met Magwitch out on the marshes. If Pip has changed since then, indeed, it has been to become hardened by his experiences—and by his expectations. Young Pip, at age seven, was at least polite to Magwitch, though Magwitch hardly seemed human to him. Now, faced with Magwitch as his benefactor, Pip loses his humanity, symbolically, as his "blood [runs] cold within him" (338, 340).

With Herbert's help, Pip learns how to respect and appreciate Magwitch and reconciles himself to some sort of responsibility to and for him. When their attempt to escape from England fails, and Magwitch is captured, Pip resolves to be his friend: "I took my place by Magwitch's side," he says, and "felt that that was my place henceforth while he lived" (456). "Please God," he promises, "I will be as true to you, as you have been to me" (457).

Magwitch's response to Pip's words is a familiar one: "I felt his hand tremble as it held mine," Pip says, "and he turned his face away . . . and I heard the old sound in his throat." Pip doesn't call it a "click" this time—he doesn't need to defend himself, by dehumanizing the sound and thus denying its meaning. He accepts it, familiarly, as he now accepts the poor man who has "felt affectionately, gratefully, and generously towards [him] with great constancy through a series of years" (456).

But Pip still has not managed to understand everything about himself or about the world. He thinks that "that old sound" is "softened now, like all the rest" of Magwitch. But Magwitch has been "softened" for some time now, by his belief in Pip's friendship. It is Pip who, grown hard with greed and pride and arrogance, has now at last been "softened."

Emotion is a difficult thing. For most of us, most of the time, the intensest emotions seem to be in some way painful: if not in themselves, then in the letdown that follows when the intensity has passed. To save ourselves from such pain, we live defensive, careful lives. The world of *Great Expectations* is very much like our world, and its inhabitants live their lives much as we do. Jaggers would prefer a life without "feelings" (427), would much rather "put the case" than admit to having experienced anything in reality. Wemmick, another conservative man, fears being seen by Jaggers as "softening" (465), and lives his public life with his face frozen in a meaningless, "mechanical," "post-office . . . smile" (196). Miss Havisham, hurt once, has stopped her life; she has raised Estella to have a "cold heart" (322), to know nothing of "sentiments and fancies" (376). Miss Havisham's excuse for her treatment of Estella is, of course, more sad defensiveness: "I meant to save her," she says, "from misery like my own" (411).

Sometimes we seem to be what Pip narrator calls "self-swindlers" (247), involved in a conspiracy against ourselves, to keep from feeling anything. To be sure, pain is not pleasure—but life, it might be argued, is feeling. And this takes us back to Joe Gargery, and the idea of "partings."

At the end of the novel, as Estella and Pip are about to part for the final time, Pip complains that "parting is a painful thing," and that their previous parting "has ever been mournful and painful" to him. Estella, however, is "glad" to part from Pip and the ruins of Satis House together. She has learned more about suffering—more about emotion itself—than Pip has. For her, "suffering has been stronger than all other teaching, and has taught [her] to understand what [Pip's] heart used to be." Having learned this, she asks that they be "friends" (493).

One might argue that friendship is an easier—safer—emotion than love. But that is neither Dickens's belief nor his point here. He argues, rather, that serious emotions last, and that the best thing we can do with our lives is to cultivate both those emotions and their continuance. "Life is made of ever so many partings welded together" is what Joe says as he shakes Pip's hand and leaves him: parts.

We shake hands—if we shake hands seriously, and not as Jaggers and Wemmick do—when we meet, or when we part: but our freedom, as friends, rarely lets us spend much of our time just holding hands. If you and I go through life together holding hands, four good hands get reduced to two—and whether we are lovers or just friends, we will starve. We will find it difficult, too, to play baseball, or ride a bike, or climb a tree. One of us may even have trouble writing, unless you're right-handed. And anyway, we are going to part eventually: that's part of the definition of life.

Early in his career Dickens had most frequently proposed as the "happy ending" of a novel that the good young people get married and raise new families of good little girls and boys. It may have been his own difficulties in marriage and in love that made him revise his ideas about happiness. He and his wife separated, in a storm of anger and recriminations, in 1858; his relationship with Ellen Ternan in the years immediately following brought him anything but happiness. If we read these bits of Dickens's biography into *Great Expectations*, we see his applying most strikingly what he learned from his own experience to make new meaning in life. But he doesn't generalize from his experience to disparage love or marriage in this novel, or in the two last novels after it. Herbert and Clara marry, as do Biddy and Joe; and there are happy marriages at the end of *Our Mutual Friend*. In *The Mystery of Edwin Drood* he writes of "love" as "the highest wisdom ever known upon this earth" (*ED*, 130). But there are no marriages in *Edwin Drood*, and in *Our Mutual Friend* the central character, Mortimer Lightwood, is left unmarried at the end. Here, Estella and Pip part, as "friends." The focus, in *Great Expectations* and after, changes for Dickens, and he looks beyond the happiness to be found in love and marriage to examine what that happiness grows from. What he discovers is that happiness grows not out of passion and possession but out of sympathetic understanding and freedom. Seeing the possibility of happiness in this new light, he enlarges his idea of the happy ending to include us all. Happiness belongs not just to the good young people who get married and begin to repopulate this sad world. It is not that we need to be replaced: rather, we need to reform ourselves. In potential at least, we are all a family together: a society—of friends.

Learning the generosity that lets us be friends is difficult, however—and maybe as dangerous as falling in love. We need to read *Great Expectations* carefully: not defensively, but carefully.

When Magwitch dies Pip is relieved of his vigil by his new friend's side. His conduct throughout Magwitch's imprisonment has been exemplary. But Pip knows that Magwitch can't live long—one way or another that will prove to be true—and thus his obligation is but a temporary one. When Magwitch dies, Pip shows us the awkward limitations of his new understanding when he prays for him: "There were no better words that I could say beside his bed, than 'O Lord, be merciful to him, a sinner!' " (470). Pip's condescension—he quotes the vain Pharisee, alas—tells us that he has not yet grown wise.[42]

Pip has three more tests after this one, before the novel closes, and all three have to do with how he treats his friends and how he understands partings. The first is with Joe, who tends him in his illness. Everything is as it was back at the forge, for a time: Joe is gentle and tender to Pip, "as if [he] were still the small helpless creature to whom [Joe] had so abundantly given the wealth of his great nature" (476). But their relationship changes as Pip recovers his health, and "the cause of [the change] was in me," Pip admits, and "the fault of it was all mine" (479).

When Joe leaves him, Pip decides to follow him to the forge and confess his wrong. But at the same time he plans to perpetrate another act of selfishness in proposing to Biddy. What he proposes to tell her is not selfish in itself. He plans to conclude, in fact, quite nobly: "And now, dear Biddy, if you can tell me that you will go through the world with me, you will surely make it a better world for me, and me a better man for it, and I will try hard to make it a better world for you" (481–82). His expectation—that of course Biddy will want him—is selfish, however, and again an indication of a limitation in Pip's understanding of the world beyond himself.

When Pip discovers that Biddy and Joe are married, he breaks down. He confesses his faults to them both, now, and begs their forgiveness. Then he departs: leaves England, to join Herbert in Cairo. Eleven years pass before he returns: "For eleven years," Pip narrator writes, "I had not seen Joe nor Biddy with my bodily eyes." But absence does not mean separation now. Like the Magwitch who had his "friend" Pip's face constantly before him out in Australia, Pip has had Joe and Biddy with him in Cairo: though he has not seen them "with [his] bodily eyes," they have "both been often before [his] fancy" (489). Parted though they have been, they have not been apart—because they are friends.

Still, "parting is a painful thing," Pip complains to Estella: "To me, the remembrance of our last parting has been ever mournful and painful." But part we must: that's what life is all about. And once Estella has made Pip tell her that they "are friends," she returns his friendship and makes that point: "And will continue friends apart."

The parting—the fact of parting—is not what is important. The friendship is the important thing. To make meaning out of Joe's difficult definition of "Life" as "made of ever so many partings welded together" we must understand the weld. The weld is what we call relationships. It shakes hands, and says "Ever the best of friends." It says "And will continue friends apart."

The weld gives us a world, a human world. And the human world, imaginatively conceived as a world of relationships, transcends both time and space, freeing us despite the limitations of human weakness and mortality.

Eleven

Guilt

As the weld of relationship creates the weightless chain that frees us, together, so the heavy chain of guilt binds us in our isolation, making relationship impossible. *Great Expectations* is a novel about both kinds of chains, and the heavy ones need to be examined as carefully as the weightless ones.

The first evidence we have in the novel of Pip's guilt or sense of guilt is presented in such a way as to suggest that the poor child has been made to feel guilty for existing from his first moment of consciousness. His sister's complaint—"It's hard enough to be a blacksmith's wife . . . without being your mother" (41)—sounds like a regular refrain the first time we hear it, partly because of the way it is said, and partly because Pip narrator couples it with her complaint about her apron— "I've never had this apron off since born you were"—which he has already told us is a constant theme with Mrs. Joe. Later he tells us that he "was always treated as if [he] had insisted on being born, in opposition to the dictates of reason, religion, and morality, and against the dissuading arguments of [his] best friends" (54).

It is not his existence, however, for which Pip feels guilt. Despite Mrs. Joe, the child Pip doesn't feel any existential guilt. But her complaint at who he is—or that he is—seems to have introduced Pip to guilt at an early age, and this perhaps causes him to exaggerate his feelings of guilt for what he does. His first crime in the novel is "larceny." As he plans it, his guilty conscience makes him see "avenging coals" in the fire (41) when he warms himself. When he asks questions—about his convict, coincidentally, though he doesn't know it yet—he is given another dose of guilt. In response to his asking "who's put into prison-ships, and why they're put there?" Mrs. Joe tells him: "People are put in the Hulks because they murder, and because they rob, and forge, and do all sorts of bad; and they always begin by

106

asking questions" (46). As he goes to bed, Pip thinks guiltily "of the great convenience that the Hulks were handy" for him.

When the time comes for him to commit his robbery, "every board . . . and every crack in every board" on the stairs at home accuse him (47), and as he runs out across the marshes "the gates and dykes and banks" all seem to cry, "as plainly as could be, 'A boy with Somebody-else's pork pie! Stop him!' "

> One black ox, with a white cravat on—who even had to my awakened conscience something of a clerical air—fixed me so obstinately with his eyes, and moved his blunt head round in such an accusatory manner as I moved round, that I blubbered out to him, "I couldn't help it, sir! It wasn't for myself I took it!" (48)

When he returns home he is filled with "remorse" for "what [his] hands had done," and suffers under the "weight" of his "wicked secret" (54–55).

Guilt is a personal thing for Pip. In order to survive at all he must reject the morality that others proclaim. If he doesn't look out for himself he might as well join his five little brothers, "who gave up trying to get a living, exceedingly early in [this] universal struggle" (35). Though Mrs. Joe's constant complaint about his existence is difficult and surely disturbing for Pip, because it is such a regular refrain it isn't really a threat to him. At the Christmas dinner, when the company "point the conversation at" him, and "stick the point into" him, he doesn't respond. He is used to being "touched up by these moral goads," it seems. When Mrs. Joe and Pumblechook try to threaten him with the need for gratitude, he resists; when Mrs. Hubble asks "Why is it that the young are never grateful?" and the answer—"Naturally wicious" (47)—is pointed at Pip, he is unmoved. When Pumblechook and Wopsle try turning their "moral" argument against the pig at him—"What is detestable in a pig, is more detestable in a boy" (58)—Pip ignores it. But throughout the dinner he feels guilty for his theft, and when Pumblechook gets his dose of brandy and tar-water Pip feels guilt instead of vindication, or the triumph of revenge. Though he is dosed with tar-water so regularly that he goes about "smelling like a new fence" (44), Pip is terrified that he has "murdered" Pumblechook (60). When Mrs. Joe goes into the pantry for the pork pie he can "bear it no more," and tries to "run away" (61). Meeting the file of soldiers at the door, he is "in an agony of apprehension" that they have come to arrest him for what he has done (62).

What guilt does is "cut off the communication"—to borrow Wemmick's phrase (229)—and turn it to another purpose. Wemmick of course never feels guilt for anything. His life is so designed as to make guilt an impossibility for him. Wemmick acknowledges no responsibility for any of his actions; thus guilt can never bother him. We might want to think that when he has raised the drawbridge and "cut off the communication" he has left the world of Little Britain behind him and can now be free and honest and honorable. What we want to think, however, and what Dickens has created for us, are in this case two different things. Even Wemmick's relationship with the Aged P. is tainted by the impersonality with which he saves himself, in Little Britain, from responsibility for his actions in life. Though "his hard face" is "really softened" when we see him "contemplating the old man," when he devotes himself to entertaining his father, Wemmick treats the Aged more like a pet to be played with than a man who is loved.

If Pip could really "cut off the communication" with Magwitch, or with Joe at the forge, he would be able—like Wemmick—to escape from the idea of guilt. But for Dickens such isolation would be dehumanizing, and could not bring Pip happiness. Safety is a very small reward in life, for Dickens. Escape to the castle—even if it were escape—would be an unsatisfactory alternative to life in the world. Since it isn't even escape, as Wemmick takes both his portable property and his principles home with him from Little Britain, it is worse. A similar escape for Pip would make him an impossible hero, for Dickens: one, most certainly, who could not have written this book for him.

Guilt interferes with communication, and makes relationships difficult. But the guilty man is still alive, in conscience, whereas the man who rejects responsibility altogether is dead to the world around him.

Wemmick never needs to wash his hands in scented soap, as the guilty Jaggers does. Jaggers fights his conscience, to be sure, and pretty effectively bullies it into submission. But Wemmick has no conscience, and is finally a worse example for Pip than was the dishonest Jaggers.

Both Wemmick and Jaggers try to avoid responsibility negatively, by means of isolation. The alternative approach to life which Dickens develops through Pip's career is the positive one that involves self-knowledge and the difficult resumption of communication with the world, called confession.

When Pip and Joe and Wopsle meet Magwitch and his captors out on the marshes, Pip tries to communicate silently with his convict, by slightly moving his hands and shaking his head (69). He wants to assure Magwitch that he is "not a deceiving imp" (50) and that Magwitch's capture is not his fault; he is afraid to speak to him, however, because he doesn't want anyone to know of his having some kind of relationship with a criminal.

It is guilt that limits Pip's communication with his convict. When Magwitch has been taken back to the Hulks and Joe and Pip have gone back to the forge, Pip still can't tell Joe—even though he and Joe are friends and fellow sufferers, and share "confidences as such" (40). The reason Pip can't tell Joe is that his fear is great and his trust limited: "The fear of losing Joe's confidence and of thenceforth sitting in the chimney-corner at night staring drearily at my for ever lost companion and friend, tied my tongue" (71–72). Pip narrator comments, generalizing from his child-self's pathetic silence to our more regular failures at communication:

> In a word, I was too cowardly to do what I knew to be right, as I had been too cowardly to avoid doing what I knew to be wrong. I had had no intercourse with the world at that time, and I imitated none of its many inhabitants who act in this manner. (72).

The next time Pip does something wrong, the situation is more complicated. When he goes to Miss Havisham's, what he does wrong is be who he is, a blacksmith's boy, with "coarse hands" and "thick boots"

(90). When Estella accuses him of having such, her "contempt" is "so strong, that it [becomes] infectious," and Pip believes her. Standing alone in the courtyard at Satis House at the end of his first day there, he takes the opportunity "to look at [his] coarse hands and [his] common boots" (91), and he finds them to be "vulgar appendages" (92). He can't admit his being "so humiliated, hurt, spurned, offended, angry, sorry" (92) to Mrs. Joe, so he tells her instead the great lie about the black velvet coach and the veal cutlets. Afterwards, however, he feels so guilty—both about the lie and about his humiliation—that he confesses to Joe. Not only does he admit that "it ain't true" about the coach and the gold plates and the dogs; he also tells Joe his frustration with his hands and boots, and his ignorance (99–100). Pip's guilt now is complex: a mixture of lies about his day at Satis House, for which he is sorry, and unhappiness about his supposed commonness, for which he can neither forgive himself nor be forgiven by Joe. Because of this he is unrelieved by his communication and continues in festering unhappiness. When he is given the two one-pound notes by the unknown man with the file—Magwitch's agent—Pip links his uncommunicated guilt about Magwitch together with his unresolved guilt about having coarse hands and rough boots, and feels "the guiltily coarse and common thing it was, to be on secret terms of conspiracy with convicts" (107–8).

Guilt grows on Pip, like weeds in a "rank garden." And just as Satis House, supposed by its name to satisfy—"whoever had [the] house, could want nothing else" (86)—does nothing of the kind for Pip or anyone else, so the weeds that grow in its garden match the weedy strangulation that is Pip's growth in the "wilderness" of his expectations. After he and Herbert fight in the garden at Satis House, Pip feels like "a species of savage young wolf," and worries that "something would be done to [him] . . . that the pale young gentleman's blood was on [his] hands, and that the Law would avenge it" (121). When Mrs. Joe is beaten, Pip immediately believes that he "must have had some hand in the attack" (147); and when it is discovered that she was attacked with a "convict's leg-iron which had been filed asunder," he blames himself for having provided the weapon, however undesignedly (148). Pip narrator recalls that for months after the crime he "suffered unspeakable trouble while [he] considered and reconsidered whether [he] should at last . . . tell Joe all the story" (148–49).

But Pip has always been treated as a guilty creature, so it is perhaps only natural that as a child he thinks himself guilty. Mrs. Joe abuses him for having been born, and the Christmas dinner party attack him with "moral goads." Later, when he is bound apprentice to Joe, Pip is dealt with "as if [he] had that moment picked a pocket or fired a rick," and a well-meaning spectator gives him a tract entitled "To Be Read In My Cell" (132). Pumblechook holds Pip as though he were a felon "on [his] way to the scaffold," and gleefully reminds everyone that Pip is "liable to imprisonment" for such crimes as playing cards, drinking, or keeping late hours (133). When Wopsle reads *George Barnwell* to Pumblechook and Pip, he performs *for* Pumblechook but *at* Pip. At the conclusion of the performance Pumblechook warns Pip solemnly, "as if it were a well-known fact that I contemplated murdering a near relation" (145).

It is Orlick, however, not Pip, who tries to murder Pip's "near relation"—and he tries, too, to murder Pip. Orlick appears rarely in the novel, but is obviously an important character in Pip's life, as Pip narrator sees it. Orlick's connection with Pip is a guilty one, in the sense that in his hideous and brutal way he mocks—mimics—so much of what Pip does. When Orlick first appears as Joe's journeyman at the forge, Pip narrator tells us that he "pretended that his christian name was Dolge—a clear impossibility" (139), and he believes Orlick "wilfully to have imposed that name upon the village as an affront to its understanding" (140). Pip's sensitivity to Orlick's having named himself correlates ironically, of course, with Pip's similar act of creating his name.

The first conflict between Pip and Orlick comes over Pip's claiming the "half-holiday" from the forge, which his articles of apprenticeship provide for, and Orlick the journeyman's demanding the same. If Pip is "going up-town," says Orlick, then "Old Orlick, *he's* a-going up-town" too (141). The result of Orlick's demand is the chain reaction that ends in his attack, that night, on Mrs. Joe. First Joe accedes to

Orlick's demand, giving "a half-holiday for all"; Mrs. Joe complains that Joe is a "fool" for "giving holidays to great idle hulkers," and she and Orlick argue. Joe and Orlick then fight; and that night Orlick attacks Mrs. Joe. Pip suspects Orlick to be her assailant (148)—but he also feels himself to be, in an indirect way, guilty of having tried to murder her!

Orlick's next crime is to be interested in Biddy. When Pip asks Biddy why she doesn't like Orlick, she replies, "because I—I am afraid he likes me." This idea makes Pip "very hot . . . as hot as if it were an outrage upon [him]self" (159). Immediately prior to his asking Biddy about Orlick, however, Pip has been explaining to her that he wishes he "could get [him]self to fall in love" with her, but can't (158). Pip's jealousy is none the less serious for his not loving Biddy: that is the mark of its selfishness. After this night, he watches Orlick carefully; were it not for Orlick's having "struck root in Joe's establishment, by reason of [Mrs. Joe's] sudden fancy for him," Pip would "have tried to get him dismissed" (159).

The next we see of Orlick he is Miss Havisham's gatekeeper (254). A quick word to Jaggers, on Pip's part—that Orlick is not "the right sort of man to fill a post of trust" (265)—gets him dismissed, and he disappears from the novel until he captures Pip out at the limekiln on the marshes. There he first accuses Pip of having cost him his place at Miss Havisham's and of having "come betwixt" himself and Biddy (435); then, more interestingly, he accuses Pip of having tried to kill Mrs. Joe. "It was you as did for your shrew sister," he says:

> I tell you it was your doing—I tell you it was done through you. . . . I giv' it her! . . . But it warn't Old Orlick as did it; it was you. You was favoured, and he was bullied and beat. Old Orlick bullied and beat, eh? Now you pays for it. You done it; now you pays for it. (437)

Pip's guilt comes home in Orlick's wild accusation. His madness makes a kind of oblique sense, one that is important for our understanding of Pip. Pip's interference between Orlick and Biddy was guilty because it was arrogant. Orlick's blaming Pip has its point: Pip did "come betwixt" them. But that's not what makes Pip's interference wrong, nor is that the point—for Dickens—of having Orlick mention it. When Biddy asked Pip not to let Orlick walk home with them, Pip "asked her why" she didn't like him:

> "Oh!" she replied . . . "because I—I am afraid he likes me."
> "Did he ever tell you he liked you?" I asked, indignantly.
> "No," said Biddy. . . . "But it makes no difference to you, you know."
> "No, Biddy, it makes no difference to me; only I don't like it; I don't approve of it."
> "Nor I either," said Biddy. "Though *that* makes no difference to you."
> "Exactly," said I; "but I must tell you I should have no opinion of you, Biddy, if he danced at you with your own consent." (159)

The wrong Pip is guilty of is the wrong he does Biddy, not Orlick; but Orlick's accusation brings it home to Pip, as guilt.

Likewise, Pip's costing Orlick his job at Miss Havisham's is not so much a crime against Orlick as it is a crime of Pip's personality. Pip is right: Orlick is not "the right sort of man to fill a post of trust at Miss Havisham's" (265). But Pip's consideration of such a fine point as "trust" is again arrogantly awkward: he has failed—and is failing— his "trust" with Joe. That same evening, when he is back in London, Pip sends Joe "a penitential codfish and a barrel of oysters." The gift serves as "reparation" for Pip (267) for not having visited Joe; and as long as he is his own judge, Pip can clear his conscience with such easy penance. Orlick's accusation reminds Pip of his own vanity, of the hollowness of his moral presumption.

The boy Pip has no reason to assume either the responsibility or the guilt for Mrs. Joe's being attacked. He knows that he didn't do it, that he has never even considered violence against her. But he has a generally guilty conscience, born out of his infatuation with Estella and the glitter of rich things at Satis House, and out of his discontent at home—and he has just spent an evening with George Barnwell. He also has that guilty secret, still, about his convict, festering inside him, and he is sure that his convict's leg-iron was the weapon used to fell Mrs. Joe.

Orlick's accusation, however, has nothing to do with these reasons for Pip's earlier feelings of guilt over the attack on Mrs. Joe. Orlick's complaint is based on Pip's having been "favoured" over him. We might well want to argue against Orlick's madness, here, that Pip was hardly "favoured" by his sister, and that Orlick was not mistreated by Joe. We can easily make the case that Orlick, in his alienation, is his own enemy. But though this kind of analysis disproves Orlick's charge, its terms set up again the awful parallel between Orlick and Pip. Though Orlick's accusation is madly twisted and false, it mimics Pip's own earlier alienated self-centeredness.

Unable to see his own shortcomings, Pip sees faults in others. Blind to his own ignorance, he plans to educate Joe. Not able to see the "bad side" of himself, he presumes to see the "bad side of human nature" in Biddy (176). He is as wrong as wrong can be, about others. But his worst wrong is what he doesn't understand about himself. It might not be too farfetched to argue that, just as Orlick's violence to Mrs. Joe doesn't hurt her—"her temper was greatly improved, and she was patient" afterwards (150)—so Pip's cruelty to Joe and Biddy doesn't hurt them. It does hurt him, however—and it's unfair to them.

It would be more comfortable for us, perhaps, if those whom Pip abuses in his arrogance as a "gentleman" would accuse him, instead of Orlick. Joe and Biddy, however, would never accuse Pip of anything, nor would Magwitch. Joe is a sort of born forgiver: he forgives his father and Mrs. Joe for their failings, and forgives Magwitch his "theft" of that pie. When asked to forgive Pip, he says, "God knows as I forgive you, if I have anythink to forgive" (488).

Pumblechook accuses Pip, but his indictments are such an outrage that they become funny. Pumblechook points at Pip and abuses him windily—but Pumblechook's morality is so false that Pip narrator berates him rather than his errant younger self. Orlick's last appearance in the novel is as the burglar who broke into Pumblechook's shop: as Joe reports it to Pip, Orlick and an accomplice "took his till, and they took his cash-box, and they drinked his wine, and they partook of his wittles, and they slapped his face, and they pulled his nose, and they tied him up to his bedpust, and they giv' him a dozen, and they stuffed his mouth full of flowering annuals" (475). This wonderful image—it is a triumph that Joe gets to create it, and recite it—makes an appropriate moral end for Pumblechook, and at the same time both completes Orlick's role as Pip's other self, doing here what Pip would have liked to do, and sends him to "the county jail" where he belongs for trying to murder Pip.

Pip can't punish Pumblechook for his falseness, partly because he has been so arrogantly false himself. At the end of the novel Pip puts up with Pumblechook's self-serving moral nonsense as quietly as he can. Pumblechook accuses him of "going to Joseph" (484), which is about the only thing he gets right in the whole novel. And as Pip goes to Joe, he makes progress and has "a sense of leaving arrogance and untruthfulness further and further behind" (486).

Aside from his own guilty conscience, Pip's arrogance has but one real accuser: Trabb's boy. Pip's first triumph as a would-be gentleman is over this "audacious boy." Mr. Trabb humbles himself before Pip's "mention" of his "handsome property" (177). Trabb "respectfully bent his body, and opened his arms," Pip narrator says, "and took the liberty of touching me on the outside of each elbow." Trabb's boy, however, is not so easily cowed into submission; he continues to sweep in spite of Pip's newly heroic emanation, and knocks his broom "against all possible corners and obstacles, to express . . . equality with any blacksmith, alive or dead" (177). Trabb threatens his boy, to prove his new loyalty to Pip's expectations, and Pip leaves the shop pleased with his "first decided experience of the stupendous power of money." It has "morally laid upon his back, Trabb's boy" (178), and Pip is arrogantly satisfied.

Trabb's boy's next appearance is a public one. Pip returns to the village to visit Satis House—not to visit Joe; when he finds himself "up and out . . . too early to go to Miss Havisham's," he wanders into the country "on Miss Havisham's side of town—which was not Joe's" (253). The morning after his visit to Satis House, as he is leaving the village—again, not to visit Joe but to return to London—he sees Trabb's boy on the High-street:

> Deeming that a serene and unconscious contemplation of him would best beseem me, and would be most likely to quell his evil mind, I advanced with that expression of countenance, and was rather congratulating myself on my success, when suddenly the knees of Trabb's boy smote together, his hair uprose, his cap fell off, he trembled violently in every limb, staggered out into the road, and crying out to the populace, "Hold me! I'm so frightened!" feigned to be in a paroxysm of terror and contrition, occasioned by the dignity of my appearance. (266)

This comically conceived tease at Pip is not the end of Trabb's boy's annoying performance, however; even its repetition, two hundred yards further along the High-street, is not the end of it. His third appearance is different from the first two, the accusation changed from a comic rendition of Pip's gentlemanly effect to a parodic representation of Pip himself:

> He . . . was strutting along the pavement towards me on the opposite side of the street, attended by a company of delighted young friends to whom from time to time he exclaimed, with a wave of his hand, "Don't know yah!"

But even this is not the worst for Pip, in his pride. Trabb's boy isn't finished with him yet:

> Words cannot state the amount of aggravation and injury wreaked upon me by Trabb's boy, when, passing abreast of me, he pulled up his shirt-collar, twined his side-hair, stuck an arm akimbo, and smirked extravagantly by, wriggling his elbows and body, and drawling to his attendants, "Don't know yah, don't know yah, pon my soul don't know yah!" (267)

Pip is outraged, and feels himself disgraced. He can't figure out, at first, how to avenge himself for the insult. The next day, however, he hits upon the appropriate gentlemanly response, and writes to Mr. Trabb "to say that Mr. Pip must decline to deal further with one who could so forget what he owed to the best interests of society, as to employ a boy who excited Loathing in every respectable mind" (267). And as a respectable companion to this letter Pip sends Joe the "penitential codfish and the barrel of oysters" aforementioned.

Pip's vengeful intention in writing to Mr. Trabb is to cost Trabb's boy his job. It is on the same visit back to the village that he causes Orlick to lose his job at Miss Havisham's. It would be overstating the connection to say that by contriving Trabb's boy's and Orlick's unemployment Pip is making them like himself. But it is true that Pip is unemployed—gentlemen shouldn't be employed!—and that he has little or no comprehension, in his current state of being, of what employment means.[43]

At the end of the novel Orlick has created new employment for himself out of his hatred for Pip. He has been working for Compeyson in London, pursuing Pip's "uncle," and now is freelancing on Pip himself. That Pip escapes the fate Orlick has planned for him is due, ironically, to Trabb's boy, who, "true to his ancient habit of happening to be everywhere where he had no business" (442), is available to serve as Herbert's guide. Luckily for Pip, Trabb's boy is "not . . . of a malignant nature" (443) and thus is willing for adventure's sake to aid Herbert.

Luckily for Pip, this world is neither as guilty nor as vengeful as he has been. Even though the world is far from being happy, or good, or whole, it is not so full of aliens as it might seem to be, or so dangerous. However hard and bad the world may be, we are often more dangerous to ourselves than it is, even at its worst. When Pip has been rescued out in the sluice-house, and saved from the limekiln, he is thankful for his life. Out of consideration for Magwitch—waiting to be taken away to France—Pip declines to pursue Orlick or cause him to be pursued: Orlick's guilt and the idea of its punishment under the law give way before the positive consideration of Pip's relationship to Magwitch and the need to save him from the law. As for Trabb's boy,

Pip gives him two guineas and apologizes for ever having "had an ill opinion of him" (443). That Orlick is a foul, mean, and brutal man is not the worst thing in the world, for Pip or for us. Pip has been worse for Pip than Orlick was, even in his threatening. And Trabb's boy has never been anything worse than what Pip's arrogance and falseness have deserved.

The greatest "swindlers" are the "self-swindlers," according to Pip narrator (247); and the greatest crimes are in some sense those that we commit against ourselves. That is the lesson of *Great Expectations*. Out of its theme of guilt and guilty conscience, out of the difficult problem of how guilt impairs communication and disturbs relationships, Dickens develops an argument for the responsible self. As Pip narrator reviews his life, confessing himself not for the cleansing purpose of confession but to teach us this lesson, he makes the roles of Orlick and Trabb's boy into important parts of his learning experience.

Twelve

Language and Other Things

Every part of Pip's life is important—for him, and by extension for us. When Biddy asks Pip if he has "quite forgotten" Estella, he answers: "My dear Biddy, I have forgotten nothing in my life that ever had a foremost place there, and little that ever had any place there" (490). Pip's assertion of memory is a particular form of the assertion of the idea of meaning—and meaning, from an imaginative point of view, is the same thing as social responsibility.

Unless life is to reduce to simple animal existence, it must have meaning. And meaning, in life, comes from the act of recollection or projective understanding. Without the possibility of meaning, human existence is nothing greater than squirrel existence—and maybe not even as great. Life for a squirrel is a matter of burying nuts and digging them up, and having a bushy tail. Nature gives the squirrel his bushy tail, in part to identify him as a squirrel. The human counterpart to the squirrel's tail is the mind: it is what identifies us as human. But the mind isn't beautiful by definition, like the squirrel's tail. We have to work at making our minds beautiful. If all we do is bury nuts and dig them up—hoard and spend, in human terms—our mindless lives won't amount to much. If we use our minds, however, to make our lives meaningful, then we will justify human existence.

When Pip thinks that Orlick is about to kill him, his active mind takes him first through thoughts "beseeching pardon" and asking for "compassion on [his]miserable errors" (437) and then, more productively, to re-created relations. In an instant, while Orlick's back is turned, Pip has "thought a prayer," and has "been with Joe and Biddy and Herbert" in his mind (439). Orlick threatens Pip with his candle, flaring it at him, "smoking [his] face and hair, and for an instant blinding [him]"—but during this instant Pip's mind defeats the threat to his body and lets him be "with Joe and Biddy and Herbert." The more Pip learns about the meaning of life, the more often his mind can serve him in this way. In the final chapter Pip narrator says upon returning to England that he "had not seen Joe and Biddy with [his] bodily eyes" for eleven years, "though they had both been often before [his] fancy in the East" (489); and when he and Estella "part," at last, it is to "continue friends apart" (493).

Great Expectations begins with Pip as a child, thinking he knows "the identity of things" (35); it concludes with his understanding the relation of things, those human relations that make meaning of life. As a child Pip determines his own identity as a thing: he sees himself out on the marshes as "a small bundle of shivers." Identifying things as things, and among things, he identifies "Pip" as but another thing, alone and alien and relationless. He is "afraid of it all"—"it all" is this world—"and beginning to cry" (36). As an adult Pip sees himself in this world, related to it by his understanding of it; and it is this understanding that lets him part from Estella at the end of the novel, trusting their friendship.

Friendship is a hard thing to learn, and perhaps even harder to learn to trust. True friendship requires nothing: it doesn't need reciprocation. Joe's friendship is always that freeing kind of relationship, from the beginning. Pip, however, finds such relationships both difficult and difficult to understand. When he is forced to part from Estella, shortly before her marriage to Drummle, Pip cries "bitter tears" (377). Insecure in himself, he can't be happy loving her unless she loves him in return. When they meet for the last time, in the "desolate garden" of what once was Satis House, Pip finds Estella "changed" and "softened," and feels "what [he] had never felt before . . . the feeling touch of the once insensible hand" (491). But merely feeling Estella's new sensitivity isn't enough for Pip, and when she tells him that they must "part" again, despite the change and the new feeling, Pip is at once disconsolate: "To me, parting is a painful thing. To me, the remembrance of our last parting has ever been mournful and painful" (493).

Estella has learned friendship now, and is free. Pip isn't so far along.

Estella tells him that he has now "a place in [her] heart": "suffering," she says, "has been stronger than all other teaching, and has taught [me] to understand what [your] heart used to be" (493). In making Pip tell her, then, that they "are friends," Estella gives him one more chance to learn this difficult lesson. "We are friends," he says; and she responds, "And will continue friends apart."

The language is simple and straightforward. Neither asks anything of the other; they both give friendship, each to the other. Pip takes her hand in his as they leave that "ruined place." If we read this gesture or act to mean that they don't part—that they don't "continue friends apart"—we read against sense, and tone, and meaning. If they can't part now, then Pip still hasn't learned what friendship is. Estella, however, has learned it, and is free. Surely Pip understands as well. If nothing else will convince us, the serenity of Pip narrator's words in the novel's final sentence should do so, as should the fact that he ends his story here:

> I took her hand in mine, and we went out of the ruined place; and, as the morning mists had risen long ago when I first left the forge, so, the evening mists were rising now, and in all the broad expanse of tranquil light they showed to me, I saw no shadow of another parting from her. (493)

Friendship isn't a bargain; it's a gift. Magwitch sees Pip's theft as a gift—and loves him for it, and tries to take the responsibility for that crime upon himself. Joe turns the theft into a wonderful Christmas gift by treating Magwitch as a "fellow-creatur" (71). But Pumblechook's Christmas presents to Mrs. Joe—"the compliments of the season" (56)—aren't gifts at all; they are silly "dumb-bell" symbols, for Pumblechook, of the power of wealth—and anyway, he and the sergeant drink both bottles!

Joe always knows what friendship is. He can't articulate it very well, however, except in poetry. "What larks!"—his standard definition of friendship—is as much a poem as his famous couplet is. Most of us speak at best but a flabby, rough prose; when we have to deal with poetry, we are likely to try to reduce it to paraphrase, to translate it down to common thought and common language. Joe works in the opposite direction. Though he is shocked to discover that he is a poet—"I never was so much surprised in all my life," he says of his couplet; "couldn't credit my own 'ed" (77)—Joe speaks poetry easily. It is that other kind of speech—the flabby, rough prose of common, uninspired thought—that he finds difficult. The language of human relations is easy for Joe; the words and gestures are one with the idea, and he is comfortable with them. Business language, however, is a very different matter for him: he is uncomfortable with its unfriendliness.

When Pip and Joe visit Miss Havisham, at her request, Joe can't speak to her. Throughout the interview he speaks only to Pip—and he prefaces his remarks with that tellingly special locution "Which I meantersay," which carries his sense of the need for direct speech as well as the impossibility of such communication, given the unfriendly restraints of both subject and situation. Miss Havisham asks Joe to identify himself—"You are the husband . . . of the sister of this boy?"—and he responds to Pip: "Which I meantersay, Pip . . . as I hup and married your sister" (128). She asks Joe if he has intended to make Pip his apprentice—and he responds to Pip. When she asks Joe if Pip likes his trade, he alters his formula slightly, saying "Which it is well known to yourself, Pip . . . that it were the wish of your own hart" (128). Does Joe have Pip's indentures with him?—"Well, Pip, you know . . . you yourself see me put 'em in my 'at, and therefore you know as they are here" (129). Does Joe expect to be paid a premium for taking Pip as an apprentice?—"Pip . . . which I meantersay . . . which you know the answer to be full well no" (129).

Even as they leave, Joe can't address Miss Havisham directly. "May you and me do our duty," he says to Pip, "both on us by one and another, and by them which your liberal present—have—conweyed—to be—for the satisfaction of mind—of—them as never—." He starts this little speech thinking in terms of duty as he reflects on the meaning of their being bound together, master and apprentice. He gets into trouble, however, when he has to direct his words and his attention toward Miss Havisham and her money, and syntax and meaning both fail him. He rescues himself with the words "and from myself far be it!"—which he repeats, for effect (130).

In his attempt to respond to Miss Havisham's questions, Joe tries twice to use his own language, and introduces his poems as answers. When she asks him if Pip has been raised to be his apprentice, Joe responds, "You know, Pip . . . as you and me were ever friends, and it were looked for'ard to betwixt us, as being calc'lated to lead to larks." When she asks if Pip likes Joe's trade, he replies with an impromptu adaptation of his couplet: "And there weren't no obligation on your part, and Pip it were the great wish of your heart" (128). The questions are questions of relations—and even under duress, terrified at the strangeness of this mad woman, Joe answers them with poetry, with the true language of relation.

The next time Joe has difficulty communicating, the topic is again one of relation—and it has to do, again, with Miss Havisham. Pip wants to pay Miss Havisham a visit; Joe thinks the idea is a bad one because "She might think you wanted something—expected something of her" (138). Pip's resistance to Joe's good advice causes him to resort to "Which I meantersay"—as a sign not so much of Joe's inarticulateness or incompetence as of the seriousness of the situation. When Pip puts his argument in terms of what he might owe her—"I have never thanked Miss Havisham," he pleads, "or asked after her, or shown that I remember her" (138)—Joe gets a new idea. The idea of Pip's giving—making—Miss Havisham a "present" gives him a better context for considering the proposal. But he can't think of an appropriate gift for Pip to make for her—and of course Pip hasn't intended to give her a present anyway. His desire to thank Miss Havisham or show her that he remembers her is a lie: he wants to see Estella.

Joe is slow, sometimes, and Pip is not at all above taking advantage of him. Honesty like Joe's isn't conditional; like friendship, it doesn't require reciprocity—and sometimes it doesn't get it. Joe lives according to principle; Pip lives according to the rule of personal desire or expedience, and thus isn't bound by honesty or by friendship.

When Jaggers comes to announce to Pip his "great expectations"

(165), he introduces the subject by asking Joe if he will give Pip his freedom, to which Joe agrees unconditionally and emphatically (164). Later, when Jaggers reintroduces the question, Joe is offended. Jaggers is more threatening than Miss Havisham, and perhaps even as strange; but Joe has no trouble talking to him directly. When Jaggers suggests that Joe may want "compensation" for the loss of Pip's "services," Joe replies:

> "Pip is that hearty welcome . . . to go free with his services . . . as no words can tell him. But if you think as Money can make compensation to me for the loss of the little child—what come to the forge—and ever the best of friends!—" (168)

When Jaggers asks the question again, Joe explodes:

> "Which I meantersay," cried Joe, "that if you come into my place bull-baiting and badgering, come out! Which I meantersay as sech if you're a man, come on! Which I meantersay that what I say, I meantersay and stand or fall by!" (168–69)

What Joe says is perfectly clear. "Which I meantersay" this time introduces what Jaggers refuses to understand. Pressed—challenged at the level of principle—Joe is thoroughly articulate, and even insistently so: "Which I meantersay that what I say, I meantersay."

Joe can express himself clearly here because Jaggers challenges his understanding of life: his values. His expostulation should have impressed Pip, but it doesn't. As Jaggers—usually the bully, but afraid of Joe—backs out the door he says, "Well, Mr. Pip, I think the sooner you leave here—as you are to be a gentleman—the better" (169). Pip should thank Joe at this point for what he has said—Pip narrator praises his "dear good faithful tender" friend (168). But the boy Pip, infatuated anew with his own prospects, does exactly what Jaggers has advised him to do: he leaves the forge—and Joe—immediately. Jaggers gives Pip a week to make up his mind, and it is in fact a week before he leaves for London; but as soon as Jaggers goes out the door

Pip "run[s] after him," deserting the forge and deserting Joe. For Joe, it is unthinkable that "Money can make compensation . . . for the loss of the little child—what come to the forge—and ever the best of friends!—" (168). For Pip, the "little child," money makes it easy to desert your values and desert your friends.

Joe knows what his life means and extrapolates in his own simple way from the ideas that organize his life to create meaning for and in the world around him. Joe's goodness is philosophically based; and if that seems a bothersomely big word for Joe, it is not such for the narrator, or for Dickens. The philosophy Joe works from is a logical and feeling one: a human and humane one. He approaches everything, it seems, with reference to some principle that he has worked out for himself. "We wouldn't have you starve to death" (71), he reassures Magwitch, thus excusing him for the supposed theft of the pie. When Pip confesses his fabrication about Miss Havisham and Satis House, Joe tells him simply that "lies is lies." (100). When he explains to Pip why he treats Mrs. Joe so kindly, the explanation is complex and most generously just—and Pip has "a new sensation" afterwards, of "looking up to Joe in [his] heart" (80) and admiring Joe's wisdom.

When Joe thinks, he thinks of others. Perhaps this proves that he is the novel's most imaginative man. The blacksmith is the artist, forging truths as well as horseshoes, making poems—about relations—as well as repairing handcuffs. The artist sees how things—or people—work together, how they relate; and meaning then becomes social.

The painter blends and juxtaposes colors, forms, and textures to make a composition. The novelist weaves together the various lives of various characters, in whatever complex circumstances he has invented as the novel's plot; the result is whole cloth. The musician makes individual notes into chords, takes themes and motifs and blends them into harmonies and symphonies. Every artist puts together whatever pieces he has to work with, to make meaning: and in this way what he does is always social.

Joe manages this kind of social work with both Mrs. Joe and Pip. He married Mrs. Joe after his parents' death: "It were but lonesome here then," he recalls, "living here alone" (77). We might think of Mrs.

Joe's contribution to Joe as many things other than the relief of his loneliness, but that is what he calls it. And when he married Mrs. Joe, he took Pip too: "God bless the poor little child . . . there's room for *him* at the forge" (78).

Joe understands how to live with Mrs. Joe: she is "given to government" (79), and he accepts this, philosophically. The alternative, as Joe sees it, is to hurt her—and his best wisdom tells him not to hurt her, or take the chance of hurting her.

Joe's relationship with Pip is also a bit of active and creative social work. Not only does he take Pip in, befriend him and protect him, he also teaches Pip. To be sure, Joe isn't "ekerval" to Pip as a "scholar"; but he knows more than Pip or anyone else in the novel about life and how to live it. When Pip narrator looks at his character-self's brief, unhappy career as Joe's apprentice, he comments on what Joe meant to him:

> It was not because I was faithful, but because Joe was faithful, that I never ran away and went for a soldier or a sailor. It was not because I had a strong sense of the virtue of industry, but because Joe had a strong sense of the virtue of industry, that I worked with a tolerable zeal against the grain. It is not possible to know how far the influence of any amiable honest-hearted duty-doing man flies out into the world; but it is very possible to know how it has touched one's self in going by. (135)

That image—of the goodness that "flies out into the world"—is a typical one, for Dickens. He seems to believe that radiance is a natural property of goodness, and in every novel from *David Copperfield* on creates characters whose goodness is thus expansive. In his early novels the character whose job is to do good in the world is typically the benevolent gentleman. This character is usually a wealthy and well-meaning older man, who does good by bestowing money upon the decent people around him. Even though Dickens gives his benevolent gentlemen seemingly unlimited wealth, they can only help a few people in their immediate world; they are incapable of any more extensive goodness, and unable to effect any sort of change in the large world.

By the time of *David Copperfield* Dickens has begun to alter his idea about how one does good in this world. As a novelist—as an artist—David has a "growing reputation and success" that "enlarge [his] power of doing good" (*DC*, 915). In *Bleak House* the benevolent gentleman, John Jarndyce, contributes money to outrageously misguided philanthropists; the good that is done in the world is that accomplished by Esther Summerson, the radiant character who tries to be "useful . . . to those immediately about [her]; and . . . to let that circle of duty gradually and naturally expand itself" (*BH*, 154). Her doctor husband also does good in the world. At the end of the novel Esther and Allan "are not much in the bank," but they do good for others and are thankful for that. Esther asks, rhetorically, "Is not this to be rich?" (*BH*, 935).

In *Great Expectations* money and goodness have very little to do with each other. The novel is full of supposed benevolences—some of them born out of good intentions—and gifts of various kinds. Mrs. Joe brings Pip up "by hand," in her hard version of generosity; Joe gives Pip a home. Miss Havisham adopts Estella; Jaggers saves Molly and gives her a place as his servant. Pip gives Magwitch food and a file; Magwitch gives Pip a fortune. A convict gives Pip two pounds, which Mrs. Joe confiscates; Miss Havisham gives Joe and Pip twenty-five pounds—which Joe cleverly gives to Mrs. Joe. Pip gives money to Herbert, and persuades Miss Havisham to add enough to his gift to buy Herbert a partnership in Clarriker's. Pip gives Joe that "penitential codfish, and a barrel of oysters." Prisoners give Wemmick all sorts of gifts—"portable property"—before they die. Even Pumblechook gives gifts, presenting Mrs. Joe with those two bottles of wine. But most of these gifts are worth little—or worthless—because they are merely gifts of money. The good gifts, in this world, are those of friendship and meaningful example.

To be sure, some gifts of money are worthy ones—because they have meaning, and are honest, exemplary acts of friendship. Pip's gift to

Herbert is one such—and Pip cries "in good earnest . . . to think that [his] expectations had done some good to somebody" (318). Magwitch's gifts to Pip are well-intentioned, too, as an expression of his love for the boy who "stood [his] friend" (360). But money doesn't radiate, for Dickens, the way goodness itself does—and goodness is thus at once the more valuable possession and the greater gift.

The goodness that radiates comes from a coherent understanding of one's self in relation to the world. Coherent understanding, indeed, is goodness, for Dickens: it is the goodness of imagination.

I have called Joe the novel's most imaginative man, its true poet. Wopsle pretends at poetry, abusing Shakespeare; Pumblechook abuses language similarly, in his windiness, though what he does is worse because he is such an abominable hypocrite. Jaggers and Wemmick both use language falsely, and they both understand the world but partially, darkly. Joe's language, on the other hand, is always honest and often colorful. It is sometimes ungrammatical, and sometimes—when he is in an uncomfortable or unnatural situation—confused. Though we can make sense of his lapses into "which I meantersay," they are usually an indication of such a stressful situation; the last one that Pip narrator records occurs on Joe's first visit to London (242–43). The most important thing about Joe's language, however, is not its wrongness or its oddness or its confusion; the important thing is the imaginative understanding that it carries. "Ever the best of friends," he says—and he knows what that assertion means, just as we do. Friendship, he says, is known "to lead to larks" (128). And "life," he says, "is made of ever so many partings welded together" (246).

Mrs. Joe doesn't think much of blacksmiths, or of the idea of the forge. When she uses the word "forge," as a matter of fact, she uses it in its other sense, of "to make falsely": "People are put in the Hulks," she says, "because they murder, and because they rob, and forge, and do all sorts of bad" (46).

But forging is a great thing, for Dickens: it is what the artist always does. And though Pip is not an artist the way David Copperfield was—Pip is a businessman, not a novelist, by profession—Pip is an imaginative person, and was so even as a child. He started out looking critically at the world, wanting to know "the identity of things." His guiltiness, as he steals food for Magwitch, is an imaginative guiltiness: he thinks he sees "a hare hanging up by the heels . . . winking" at him (47) in the pantry, and out on the marshes he meets a "black ox, with a white cravat on—who even had to my awakened conscience something of a clerical air" (48). When he first visits Miss Havisham's, he puts together what he sees there and creates that wonderfully imaginative and meaningful lie about the black velvet coach and the gold plates—and the swords, and the jam, and the pills.

Pip's greatest achievement in the imaginative line, however, is his achievement as the narrator of this story. In the way he organizes his life into meaning, not just for himself but as a moral lesson for us, he is the best artist. And through this work his "influence . . . flies out into the world," too, just as Joe's does.

Thirteen

Conclusion

"The world," in *Great Expectations*, is in some ways as big as it ever gets in Dickens's fiction. It isn't just that Pip goes off to Cairo to work; Dickens's characters have never been restricted geographically. Nor is it that "the world" had grandly mythic dimensions, borrowed from Milton, as Pip leaves his village for London. Though "the mists [have] all solemnly risen . . . and the world lay spread before [him]" (186), the vista quickly enough contracts, and he finds himself at the end of a five-hour coach ride at "the Cross Keys, Wood-Street, Cheapside, London" (187).

Still, the world of *Great Expectations* is a large world—and this is true though its canvas is smaller than that of the great monthly-part novels like *David Copperfield, Bleak House, Little Dorrit,* and *Our Mutual Friend. Great Expectations* is slightly more than half as long as Dickens's full-length novels, and contains but a handful of characters by comparison with them. Its largeness is due to Pip's understanding of himself, and to the generosity of soul with which he presents himself to us. And however limited in size this novel is, it is great for these reasons.

Great Expectations is a solemn novel, but it is also a comic novel. It is a dramatic novel that contains the human world in all its varieties, seen by a compassionately successful inhabitant of it. Because its most general and comprehensive theme concerns relationships, one of the ways the novel works is through its representation of Pip's many relationships. His relationships become the complex upon which the novel is built and through which we see or feel both its seriousness and its humor.

The first point of Pip's relationships is that he doesn't just *know* the various characters in the novel; he is positively related to them all. The novel begins with his enumeration of several failed relationships: his father and mother are "dead and buried," as are his five little brothers "who gave up trying to get a living, exceedingly early in that universal struggle" called life (35). His sister raises him, "by hand" and against her will. Her husband, however, teaches Pip friendship: "Ever the best of friends," he says. And that starts Pip on the road to relating himself to this world. Magwitch scares him, but he becomes in the boy Pip's mind "my convict"—though Pip has no idea what it means to claim a relationship with such a man. Pip is "fearfully sensible" that he is on his way toward being a criminal, though he doesn't put himself together with Magwitch when he feels or thinks this. It is only after he has met Miss Havisham and Estella—and formed his relationships with them—that he thinks "of the guiltily coarse and common thing it was, to be on secret terms of conspiracy with convicts" (108).

But Pip and Magwitch are related, and they are in many ways alike: as aliens, as prisoners, as criminals, as—when Magwitch was a boy—orphans who must fend for themselves. Eventually, because Pip has befriended his convict, Magwitch all but adopts him: "I'm your second father," he tells Pip: "You're my son—more to me nor any son" (377).

Pip is also related to Pumblechook, and has an odd connection with Mr. Wopsle as well. Wopsle is another creature who is being kept down; if only the Church were "thrown open" to competition, he would surely prove his worth (55). Dissatisfied with his life as a mere clerk in the Church, he eventually renounces religion and runs away—like Pip, to London—to seek his fortune as an actor. In one of his early forays into the world of the theater, he captures Pip to "read at" (144)—and does George Barnwell at him. Pip acquiesces because Wopsle will walk him home afterwards: "the nights were dark and the way dreary, and almost any companionship on the road was better than none" (144).

When Pip narrator introduces Pumblechook, he explains that the two of them are not in fact related. "Uncle Pumblechook" is Joe's uncle, not Mrs. Joe's; further, Pip is "not allowed to call him uncle, under severest penalties" (55). During the course of the novel Pip narrator regularly calls Pumblechook an "ass," a "windy donkey," an "imposter," and a "hypocrite." He is also "that basest of swindlers" (133), "that swindling Pumblechook" (134), when he pretends to have been consulted by Miss Havisham about her gift to Pip. "Swindler" is a slightly odd word to substitute for "liar" here; in its oddness it provides, perhaps a clue to Pip's extreme animosity toward Pumblechook and an insight into their relation.

Not that Pumblechook doesn't deserve to be called names, of course. He is, absolutely, an ass and an imposter and a hypocrite and all the other nasty things Pip narrator calls him, including swindler. He is a stupid, greedy man who worships money. He enjoys being respected by those who are not as affluent as he is—he keeps his own shay-cart, after all!—and fawns on those who are more so. His attitude toward Pip once he has "expectations" is an example of his swindling dishonesty; its counterpart is his "forgiving" attitude toward the fallen Pip.

But Pumblechook's values are not unlike what someone else's once were. And when we hear Pip narrator complain of his own younger self's swindling—"All other swindlers upon earth are nothing to the self-swindlers," he says (247)—we should begin both to associate Pumblechook with Pip, awkwardly, and to understand Pip narrator's antagonism to that shameful man.[44] Pip the "self-swindler" uses "such pretenses"to "cheat [him]self." Swindling isn't as easy for Pip, however, as it is for Pumblechook. Pumblechook is so coarse and selfish and vulgar that swindling seems to come naturally to him. But Pip works at it: actually works to cheat himself. As he grows accustomed to his expectations, he begins "insensibly . . . to notice their effect upon [him]self and those around [him]." But the swindler in him avoids examining what "insensibly" he has begun to know: "Their influence on my own character, I disguised from my recognition as much as possible" (291).

What saves Pip, of course, is that he is not a Pumblechook at heart. He is not such a selfish and self-serving beast. He has a conscience, which means that though he "disguised" the effect of his expectations "as much as possible," still he "knew very well that it was not all good." And thus, he says, "I lived in a state of chronic uneasiness respecting my behavior to Joe. My conscience was not by any means comfortable about Biddy" (291).

Pip's relationship with Biddy begins with her being "an orphan, like myself" who "like me . . . had been brought up by hand." Pip narrator furthers the relationship by telling us about Biddy's hands and feet: her hands are not "coarse," like Pip's, but they "always wanted washing"; her boots, though not "rough," "always wanted mending and pulling up at the heel" (74). Later, Pip wants to fall in love with Biddy, but can't; toward the end of the novel he wants to marry her, but must learn instead to be her friend.

In his innocence and newness to London, Pip tries to be friends with both Jaggers and Wemmick, but they are men who don't allow feelings, or relations, or communications in their professional lives, and thus lead restricted, defensive, and finally unfriendly domestic lives. Pip doesn't like Bentley Drummle, ever; but Pip narrator recalls two scenes in which, for all of his younger self's protests against Drummle, the two act remarkably alike. The first takes place among the Finches of the Grove, when Drummle proposes a toast to Estella. Pip is outraged, and in a wonderfully silly exchange almost challenges Drummle to a duel. The Finches intervene, however, bargaining for Drummle's proving that he has a right to toast Estella—which he does. Pip apologizes, and then the two young fools sit "snorting at one another for an hour" (327). The second scene takes place at the Blue Boar, in Pip's village. Pip and Drummle are both in town, awkwardly, to visit Estella.

> As he pretended not to see me, I pretended not to see him. It was a very lame pretence on both sides; the lamer, because we both went into the coffee-room, where he had just finished his breakfast, and where I ordered mine. . . .
>
> Pretending to read a smeary newspaper . . . I sat at my table while he stood before the fire. By degrees it became an enormous injury to me that he stood before the fire, and I got up to have my share of it. . . .
>
> "You have just come down?" said Mr. Drummle, edging me a little away with his shoulder.

"Yes," said I, edging *him* a little away with *my* shoulder. . . .

Here Mr. Drummle looked at his boots, and I looked at mine, and then Mr. Drummle looked at my boots, and I looked at his. . . .

"Do you stay here long?"

"Can't say," answered Mr. Drummle, "Do you?"

"Can't say," said I.

I felt here, through a tingling in my blood, that if Mr. Drummle's shoulder had claimed another hair's breadth of room, I should have jerked him to the window; equally, that if my shoulder had urged a similar claim, Mr. Drummle would have jerked me into the box. He whistled a little. So did I. . . .

One thing was manifest to both of us, and that was, that until relief came, neither of us could relinquish the fire. There we stood, well squared up before it, shoulder to shoulder and foot to foot, with our hands behind us, not budging an inch. (368–70)

Pip would prefer not to be related to Orlick or to Trabb's boy, but he is related to both, as we have seen. In a telling coincidence, he and Orlick both name themselves. When Orlick attacks Mrs. Joe, Pip blames himself though he suspects Orlick; later, out on the marshes, Orlick blames Pip directly for what he himself has done. The last we hear of Orlick he is in jail for having done what Pip would have liked to do: he has assaulted Pumblechook (475). In his first confrontation with Trabb's boy, Pip sees this youngster as asserting his "equality with any blacksmith" and resents this (177). Later, Trabb's boy mimics Pip, re-creating himself as a mock-gentleman and accompanying Pip down the High-street (266–67).

Pip's most important relationships, of course, are the chosen relationships: the real and intentional ones, the ones that end in friendship. All the others are but suggestions toward the larger theme, reminders to us that relationship is life, finally and absolutely, and that we must make the best relationships we can.

We all need relationships. When Pumblechook and Pip part—Pip is "going to Joseph" to reaffirm that relationship—Pumblechook is not left alone: "imposter" that he is, he collects a "select group" of villagers to tell his story to. When Mrs. Joe has been injured, she changes completely. Though "her temper [is] greatly improved" (150) her "sight [is] disturbed . . . her hearing . . . greatly impaired; her memory also; and her speech . . . unintelligible" (149). Sometimes Pip narrator says, "she would . . . put her hands to her head, and would remain for about a week at a time in some gloomy aberration of mind" (150). But Mrs. Joe is not totally alone, even in her new mental isolation: she asks, almost every day, for Orlick's company (151). What keeps Miss Havisham alive is not her loneliness or her revenge, but her companionship with Estella. Once that is broken—once Estella proves to her that there is no relationship between them—she has nothing to live for. Her use of Pip is also a demonstration of her inability to survive alone; her resolution of that use—by asking his forgiveness—is what enables her to die more like a human being than she has let herself live.

The best relationships are those between Pip and Joe, Pip and Herbert, Joe and Biddy, and finally Pip and Estella. They are the relationships of love and friendship which Dickens so valued, and upon which he proposed that we should build our lives. In his last novel, *The Mystery of Edwin Drood*, he writes that "Love . . . is the highest wisdom ever known upon this earth" (*ED*, 130). For Dickens, certainly, that is the first and most important truth of human existence. It is at once the most serious lesson he can offer us, his best and highest wisdom, and at the same time the most delightful of simple pleasures. The countersign to "Love . . . is the highest wisdom ever known upon this earth" is "What larks!"

When, at the end of *Great Expectations*, Pip and Estella leave "the ruined place" that once was Satis House, the tone is serious and solemn. As "the evening mists" rise now, they speak not of "beginning the world" (*BH*, 920), as the morning mists did when they "had all solemnly risen" when the young adventurer Pip set out for London with "the world . . . spread before [him]" (186). Rather, the evening mists rise to reveal a later world in a "broad expanse of tranquil light" (493). The tone is solemn, as the novel closes. What it closes on is a whole world: a world made whole by the comprehensive quality of Pip narrator's understanding of it and relations in it. As we finish our reading, we must keep the whole in mind: and we must not forget, in the seriousness of its conclusion, the wonderful comedy that it contains.

Great Expectations is comic because Pip narrator can make it so. Wemmick is a wonderful comic character despite his corruption, because Pip narrator understands him: and understanding is greater than judgment. Mrs. Joe's meanness is comic not only because Pip survived it, but because Pip narrator understands it and has learned from it. Joe remains beautifully comic, even when Pip character abuses him, because Pip narrator respects Joe and knows how to love him. The same is true of Herbert.

Magwitch and Miss Havisham are not comic, however, though their grotesqueries are almost so. But the way in which Pip narrator comes to deal with Miss Havisham and Magwitch is related to what I have just been talking about as comedy. The general heading for what I want to argue here, at the end of our discussion of *Great Expectations*, might be something like "Sympathy Legitimizes Laughter," or "Understanding Sets Us Free."

The novel records carefully and explicitly scenes in which Pip character learns to sympathize with Magwitch and Miss Havisham. Both are significant scenes. In each Pip learns a truth about himself while learning sympathy for another. What Pip has learned in learning to love Magwitch shows in Pip narrator's representation of their first scenes together, which though terrifying to the boy Pip are comic to his recollecting narrative self. What he has learned from his sympathy for Miss Havisham—"compassion" and "pity" are the words Pip narrator uses—appears tellingly in a small detail toward the end of the novel. The last time he visits Satis House before it is "pulled down" (482) he sees "the wheeled chair [he] had so often pushed along to the tune of Old Clem" (483). There is nothing of bitterness or blame or remorse in the sight, or in its recollection. That the recollection identifies the chair with his and Miss Havisham's singing "Old Clem" underlines Pip's peace, his acceptance and understanding of his past, and makes of the image something sweet and almost comic.

Comedy, finally, comes from seriousness. Wholeness is itself a kind of laughter. Love is the mysterious forgery that enables mortals to laugh, even at death.

Friendship, as Joe knew all along, is "calc'lated to lead to larks" (121). And however serious this world is, that seriousness must include Joe's larks. If friendship means relationship—as well as freedom—and relationships hold this world together, then we are free, as friends, to laugh and enjoy everything: everything that we comprehend, everything that in our best seriousness we put together to call life.

Student Responses
to Great Expectations

The following brief comments were written by students in my *Great Expectations* class at the University of Michigan in the winter of 1985. The course was a large lecture course; to overcome the problem of size—so that the students could all talk, and so that I could talk with them—they wrote "scribbles" for five minutes at the end of each class. I collected these, read them, scribbled back in response, and returned them to the students at the start of the next class. I have chosen a small sampling of what seemed to me the best ones: the most thoughtful ones, the ones that perhaps Dickens would have been proud to have provoked in his students.

· · ·

One thing that has occurred to me as I've been reading the book for the second time is that my view of Pip is changing. After finishing the novel the first time I thought that Pip was the most unfortunate character in it, one whose life had been ruined. He didn't even get the girl at the end. But now that I think about it, he doesn't really end up in such a bad way after all. He has learned his lesson in that he knows being a gentleman will not make him happy. Only friendship and affection can do that. In this way he is a lot better off than Jaggers or Wemmick. Perhaps he is not as sad a character as I first thought. It's too bad that he had to learn it all the hard way—but isn't that what life is often all about?

—*Jon Bokar*

Pip comes to see knowledge not as understanding the manners of gentlemen but as understanding other people's hearts and doing good with them. Knowledge gained in a university should not be used for the accumulation of wealth—class ring equals a Rolls Royce—because the more you own in "portable property" the less someone else can have. And if "portable property" is the measure of happiness, then there's a limit to human happiness: there's only so much to go around.

There is a limited amount of "portable property" in this world. But none of us needs very much of that stuff, really, so there's enough. What we need lots of is happiness. Real happiness.

—*Adam Ruskin*

Dinners. Looking at Jaggers hosting that dinner for Pip and his friends, and controlling everything from the conversation to the sauces and liquors he dispenses from the dumb waiter, I remember other meals in the novel. The Aged P. and his toast and sausages. Pip and Herbert, on their own. Magwitch, eating like an animal—and Pip in his new manners repulsed by the way Magwitch feeds. Pip and Joe at tea, and their game with their bread. Pip, alone in the garden at Satis House, eating scraps. And the Christmas dinner at the Forge, which had nothing at all to do with Christmas. And that lovely meal that Pip gives Magwitch out on the marshes—a real Christmas dinner, in every way!

Dickens makes a lot of sense out of the novel by the way he shows us people eating. I guess that's appropriate: meals are times not just for feeding our bodies, but communion times, times for relating ourselves to each other.

—*Helen Thomas*

It would be amazing if everyone could reach out and be affected by companionship. Even the hardest times can be made easier. An example of this is that even in the short experience in the graveyard Magwitch's tone of voice with Pip changes, along with his attitude.

He never realizes that Pip came out of fear, and the thought—the imagination—that someone would do something nice for him affects and softens him.

Companionship and compassion are essential, no matter what you do in life.

—*Stephanie Grodin*

The contrast between Magwitch's and Jaggers's attitudes toward friendship really makes me stop and think about what kind of people are truly happy. I discovered that those people who appreciate the simple things in life, such as a meal shared with a friend, are the happy ones. Jaggers never knows the great feeling you get when you share with others—and that's what makes him the character to be pitied, not Magwitch.

—*Christine O'Neil*

Many people go through life walking on their real friends and building up false ones. Some never realize that this has happened until it's too late.

—*John Roedin*

Magwitch determines a gentleman by his possessions. Likewise he believes that money should determine class. But so what? That's what we do today. We don't determine class by identifying those who have kind hearts and help others in need. No, we determine class by wealth and wealth alone. It doesn't matter what your education. It doesn't matter what your integrity. All that matters is how much money you have and how much more you can earn. What Dickens shows us in Magwitch's idea of class is actually what we as a society think class is. Though Dickens wrote this many years ago, this false idea of class is still with us.

—*John Roedin*

The education of Pip provides insight into the education of young people today. We don't value individuals like Joe who provide the world with simple understanding and immense human compassion. When I ask my younger brother and sister who their heroes are, my brother will point to sports stars and my sister to actors and musicians. When I probe further I find the reason for their choices: money.

—*Vivek Vasudeva*

I have been doing a great deal of thinking which is nearly parallel with your idea of *Great Expectations* as a novel which is subversive in our time. Why do so many of us attend college? Is it for wisdom? For knowledge? Or merely because we have heard our parents say that this is the only way to get a good job, to get ahead in this world? Having such motivations and ambitions, will any of us become like Pip and forget our former friends and so-called humbler beginnings? Could we forget the Joes in our lives?

Yes, *Great Expectations* examines today's social values in detail, and it raises some questions that everyone should examine. It's easy to see Pip's mistakes in the novel, but can we see our own in real life?

—*Sue Pahl*

One important theme of *Great Expectations* which still applies today is that money does not bring a person happiness. Pip wants to become a gentleman and win Estella's love, and he believes that all he has to do to achieve these ends is get money and an education. But when he gets both of these—his "great expectations"—he is not happy, partly because he has left behind him Joe and Biddy, his true friends.

This theme really applies today. Our society is very materialistic. We go to school to get an education so we can get a good-paying job and buy all the material objects that will make us happy. Maybe we should all read *Great Expectations*—so that we could avoid all the pain and heartache Pip brought upon himself.

—*Jeff Kidd*

As you were talking about the subversiveness of the novel, I was struck by what seems like an obvious question, but one which I hadn't thought about before. If Pip narrator is happy and good and right about things—as Joe is—why are so many of us in this educated world still pre-education Pips? Why do we take incompetence and hypocrisy for granted, and scoff at "idealistic kids" who are "fools" for being idealistic? At one o'clock today, it doesn't make a whole lot of sense.

—*Mike Cramer*

I hadn't really thought of *Great Expectations* as a subversive attack on our money-oriented society before I took this class. Before, it was pure entertainment for me. Now it is a bit disturbing. The first time I read the novel I sympathized with Wemmick and admired his lifestyle. I actually agreed with him that it was a shame to lose that perfectly good portable property when Magwitch died. Of course, Pip's friendship with Magwitch was more important than the property, but would Pip's acquiring the property have ruined their relationship? I don't think so. I think that Magwitch would have wanted Pip to have the property.

I guess my values are too deeply rooted in our materialistic society. I understand your point about Wemmick's insincerity in living such a double life, and I definitely wouldn't want to be just like Wemmick, but I don't think I can help understanding his position. I see some of Wemmick in myself, and in almost everyone around me. What's worse, I'm headed for law school next year—so I may end up like Mr. Jaggers!

—*Joe Shea*

It must be some kind of bug that bites most of us in life, making us want to rise in our society for no other reason than glitter. It's a shame that we use our education for that purpose—and end up not learning anything at all. Pip was fortunate enough to get over that sting and begin to live a real life.

I am planning a career in medicine, and I hope I will be able to reject the Grosse Pointe office for something truly valuable. If you ever see me in an office there, please give me a kick in the behind.

—*John Swirzcek*

One of the most delightful aspects of reading Dickens is to read with ravenous appetite an adventure story, only to realize that I have been internalizing something that moves me to the core. That something is a moral lesson.

—*Mary Sickler*

Notes

1. J.C. Jeaffreson, *Novels and Novelists*; quoted by George H. Ford, in *Dickens and His Readers* (New York: W. W. Norton, 1965), 100.

2. Letter to John Forster; quoted in John Forster, *The Life of Charles Dickens*, (New York: E. P. Dutton & Co., 1948), Everyman edition, 2:284.

3. *Times* (London), 17 October 1861, 6.

4. *Athenaeum*, 13 July 1861, 45.

5. *Eclectic Review* 114 (October 1861), 467, 471.

6. *Athenaeum*, 13 July 1861, 43.

7. *Blackwood's Magazine* 55 (May 1862), 565.

8. *Rambler*, January 1862, 276.

9. Forster, *Life*, 2:285.

10. Ibid., 286–87.

11. Ibid., 287.

12. Edwin P. Whipple, "Dickens's *Great Expectations*," *Atlantic Monthly* 8 (September 1877), 328.

13. G. K. Chesterton, *Criticisms and Appreciations of Charles Dickens* (New York: E. P. Dutton & Co. 1911), 197.

14. Ibid., 199.

15. Ford Madox Ford, *The March of Literature from Confucius to Modern Times*; quotes in *Dickensian* 37 (1940):113–14.

16. Edgar Johnson, *Charles Dickens: His Tragedy and Triumph* (New York: Simon & Schuster, 1952), 2:989.

17. J. Hillis Miller, *Charles Dickens: the World of His Novels* (Cambridge, Mass.: Harvard University Press, 1958), 278.

18. Ibid., 277.

19. Dorothy Van Ghent, *The English Novel: Form and Function* (New York: Holt, Rinehart, & Winston, 1953), 138.

20. Julian Moynahan, "The Hero's Guilt: The Case of *Great Expectations*," *Essays in Criticism* 10 (January 1960):78.

21. Ibid., 79.

22. Forster, *Life*, 2:284.

23. Ibid.

24. Ibid., 285.

25. Ibid.

26. Samuel Taylor Coleridge, *Biographia Literaria* (1817), chap. 13.

27. Dickens to Wilkie Collins, 6 September 1858.

28. Anthony Trollope, "Charles Dickens," *St. Paul's Magazine* 6 (1870):374.

29. Forster, *Life*, 2:183.

30. See Adam Ruskin, "Ford's Deceptive Address," *Michigan Daily*, 17 January 1985, 4. See also *Detroit News*, 23 January 1985, and *Ann Arbor News*, 24 January 1985.

31. Fyodor Dostoievski, *Notes from Underground* (Crowell edition), 39.

32. Ralph Ellison, *Invisible Man* (New York: Random House, 1972 Vintage edition), 566.

33. George Eliot, quoted in Thomas Pinney, "More Leaves from George Eliot's Notebook," *Huntington Library Quarterly* 22 (1966):364.

34. George Eliot to Charles Bray, 5 July 1859, in *The George Eliot Letters*, ed. Gordon S. Haight (New Haven: Yale University Press, 1954), 3:111.

35. Miss Havisham hired Jaggers, indeed, to shut her out from the world (*GE*, 412).

36. Forster printed the original as a footnote in his *Life*. It was first printed as the conclusion to the novel by G. B. Shaw in his text for the Limited Editions Club in 1937. Both endings are usually printed in modern editions, with the ending that Dickens canceled included in an appendix.

37. Joel J. Brattin—the erstwhile student of whom I speak—has written about this matter in his Stanford University dissertation, "Reading Between the Lines: Dickens's Later Manuscripts" (1985).

38. G. B. Shaw, Preface to *Great Expectations*, Limited Editions Club.

39. Charles R. Forker has written an essay on "The Language of Hands in *Great Expectations*," *Studies in Literature and Language* 3 (1961):280–91.

40. *Macbeth*, act 5, sc. 1, lines 48–49.

41. *Biographia Literaria*, chap. 13.

42. Critics have argued about this line in many different ways. The manuscript version is clean. I find it difficult to believe that Dickens intended the irony which Pip's misappropriation of the biblical text (Luke 18:10–14) creates. Still, Pip does say it—or quotes himself as saying it. And his mistake is very awkward, to say the least.

43. When Pip goes back to the village for his sister's funeral he looks about among "Trabb and his men" for the boy, but doesn't find him—presumably because he is no longer in fact "Trabb's boy" (*GE*, 301).

44. I am indebted to David Scott, a student in my Dickens class in 1985, for showing me this connection.

Bibliography

Primary Sources

Great Expectations was first published in the weekly numbers of *All the Year Round*, from 1 December 1860 (No. 83) to 3 August 1861 (no. 119). It was issued in a single volume by Chapman and Hall in 1861. The manuscript of *Great Expectations* is in the Wisbech and Fenland Museum at Wisbech, Cambridgeshire. The proof sheets are at the Pierpont Morgan Library in New York.

The standard editions of the *Letters of Charles Dickens* are the Nonesuch edition, in three volumes, edited by Arthur Waugh et al. (1938), and the Pilgrim edition, in progress, edited by Madeline House and Graham Storey (1965–).

Secondary Sources

Reviews of *Great Expectations*

Athenaeum, 13 July 1861, 43–45.
Blackwood's Magazine 55 (6 May 1861):564–84.
Eclectic Review 114 (October 1861):458–77.
Rambler, January 1862, 274–76.
Saturday Review 12 (July 1861):69–70.
Times (London), 17 October 1861, 6.

Biographies of Dickens

FORSTER, JOHN. *The Life of Charles Dickens*. 3 vols. London: Chapman and Hall, 1872–74. Reprinted by E. P. Dutton and Co. in Everyman Library, 2 vols, 1927, 1948.

JOHNSON, EDGAR. *Charles Dickens: His Tragedy and Triumph*. 2 vols. New York: Simon and Schuster, 1952. Reprinted in 1982 without the excellent critical chapters.

Criticism of *Great Expectations*

AXTON, WILLIAM F. "*Great Expectations Yet Again.*" *Dickens Studies Annual* 2 (1972):278–93.

CHESTERTON, G. K. "*Great Expectations.*" *Criticisms and Appreciations of Charles Dickens.* New York: E.P. Dutton & Co., 1911. Pp. 197–206.

DALESKI, H. H. "*Great Expectations.*" In *Dickens and the Art of Analogy.* London: Faber and Faber, 1970. Pp. 237–70.

DUNN, ALBERT A. "The Altered Endings of *Great Expectations*: A Note on Bibliography and First-Person Narrative."*Dickens Studies Newsletter* 9 (1978):40–42.

ENGLE, MONROE. "The Sense of Self." *The Maturity of Dickens.* Cambridge, Mass.: Harvard University Press, 1959. Pp. 146–68. An excellent essay comparing *Great Expectations* and *David Copperfield.*

FORD, GEORGE H. *Dickens and His Readers.* Princeton, N. J.: Princeton University Press, 1955. Reprint. New York: W. W. Norton, 1965. A rich and readable account of Dickens's fiction and its critical reception.

FORKER, CHARLES R. "The Language of Hands in *Great Expectations.*" *Studies in Literature and Language* 3 (1961):280–93.

GOLD, JOSEPH. "You Make Your Own Snares." In *Charles Dickens, Radical Moralist.* Minneapolis: University of Minnesota Press, 1972. Pp. 241–54.

HARDY, BARBARA. "*Great Expectations.*" In *The Moral Art of Dickens.* London: Athlone Press, 1970. Pp. 139–55. A lovely meditation on the meaning of food in *Great Expectations.*

HILL, T. W. "*Great Expectations.*" *Dickensian* 53 (May 1957):119–26; 53 (September 1957):184–86; 54 (January 1958):53–60; 54 (May 1958):123–25; 54 (September 1958):185; 55 (January 1959):57–59; 56 (May 1960):121–26.

JACKSON, THOMAS A. *Charles Dickens, the Progress of a Radical.* New York: International Publishers, 1938. Pp. 192–200.

LEAVIS, Q. D. "How We Must Read *Great Expectations.*" In *Dickens the Novelist* by F. R. and Q. D. Leavis, 272-331. London: Chatto and Windus, 1970. A large, thoughtful, sometimes crotchety, and informative study of the novel.

LETTIS, RICHARD, and WILLIAM MORRIS. *Assessing Great Expectations.* San Francisco: Chandler Publishing Co. 1960. A useful collection of reviews and essays.

MILLER, J. HILLIS. "*Great Expectations.*" In *Charles Dickens: The World of His Novels.* Cambridge, Mass.: Harvard University Press, 1958. Pp. 249–78. An excellent essay, in one of the most important books on Dickens.

MOYNAHAN, JULIAN. "The Hero's Guilt: The Case of *Great Expectations*." *Essays in Criticism* 10 (1960):60–79.

PAGE, NORMAN. *Hard Times, Great Expectations, Our Mutual Friend: A Casebook*. London: Macmillan & Co., 1979.

ROSENBERG, EDGAR. "A Preface to *Great Expectations*." *Dickens Studies Annual* 2 (1972):294–335. A delightful, meandering essay by a knowledgeable scholar.

SHAW, GEORGE BERNARD. Introduction to *Great Expectations*. (Limited Editions Club). Edinburgh, 1937.

STOEHR, TAYLOR. "The Novel as Dream: *Great Expectations*." *Dickens: The Dreamer's Stance*. Ithaca, N. Y.: Cornell University Press, 1965. Pp 101–37.

TROLLOPE, ANTHONY. "Charles Dickens." *St. Paul's Magazine* 6 (1870): 374. A brief but significant obituary notice.

VAN GHENT, DOROTHY. "On *Great Expectations*." *The English Novel: Form and Function*. New York: Holt, Rinehart, & Winston, 1953. Pp. 125–38. An important essay, exploring Dickens's use of imagery and the themes of guilt and redemption.

Index

The nature of this book is such that to index thematic material would be self-defeating: "friendship," "money and wealth," "social criticism," "education," and "imagination," for example, appear in some form on almost every page. The same is true of the major characters in *Great Expectations*. This index, therefore, is limited to references (1) to Dickens's works, excluding *Great Expectations*, and (2) to other writers and thinkers mentioned in the text.

About the Author

Bert G. Hornback is a professor of English at the University of Michigan in Ann Arbor. Among his books are three on Charles Dickens: "*Noah's Arkitecture*": *A Study of Dickens's Mythology* (1972), "*The Hero of My life*": *Essays on Dickens* (1981), and *Our Mutual Friend: An Annotated Bibliography* (with Joel J. Brattin, 1984). He wrote and acted in a ten-part television series, *The Dickens World*, produced in 1973. He is the founder and secretary of the Ann Arbor branch of the International Dickens Fellowship, and has served as a Trustee of the Dickens Society of America. Since 1977 he has re-created Dickens's famous dramatic readings for audiences all over America.

Hornback is the former director of the Great Books Program at the University of Michigan, director of the Center for the Advancement of Peripheral Thought, and the founder of the Society of Bremen Scholars. He spends most of his time teaching undergraduates, and has been honored three times by the University of Michigan for his excellence in the classroom and as an Honors academic advisor.